The Trail

THE TRAIL

A Bibliography of the
Travelers on the
Overland Trail to California,
Oregon, Salt Lake City,
and Montana
during the Years
1841–1864

by Lannon W. Mintz

University of New Mexico Press
Albuquerque

Library of Congress Cataloging-in-Publication Data

Mintz, Lannon W., 1938–
  The trail: a bibliography of the travelers on the
overland trail to California, Oregon, Salt Lake City, and
Montana during the years 1841–1864.

  Includes index.
  1. West (U.S.)—Description and travel—To 1848—
Bibliography.   2. West (U.S.)—Description and
travel—1848–1860—Bibliography.   3. West (U.S.)—
Description and travel—1860–1880—Bibliography.
4. Overland journeys to the Pacific—Bibliography.
I. Title. Z1251.W5M56   1987   [F592]   016.9178
86-25117
ISBN 0-8263-0939-9

To Jack Rittenhouse
    whose assistance and counsel
        helped to make this journey possible.

Contents

Preface

This bibliography was vigilantly assembled with the book dealer, the librarian, the book collector, and the many amateur and professional students of our country's history in mind. Included here are the "collectible" diaries, journals, letters, and reminiscences of those participating in this nation's most heroic, and most romantic, mass adventure. Again and again, we the reader can become vicariously immersed in the exacting and often times disastrous enterprise. Hundreds of different accounts, related from an endless variety of perspectives, furnish all those pondering the history of the movement West with an endless supply of comparative experiences and a panorama of the event itself.

Two distinctions are common to each of the entries. The journey to the West was along the northern road to Oregon and California, by way of the Platte River, Fort Laramie, and the South Pass through the Rockies. And, the participants' firsthand account of the event was recorded by them, or by someone who knew them.

The entries included here are for the years 1841, the year of the first overland emigrant train, to the fall of 1864. The participants are listed alphabetically. The travelers encompass everyone who trod west along this route, from the enterprising Fremont to the relatively unknown G. C. Pearson, or Phoebe G. Judson.

The major destinations of the westward bound are all represented here: Oregon, where land offered a new life; California, where gold meant opportunity, and perhaps success; Salt Lake City, offering religious sanctuary; and the Virginia City area of Montana with its enticing lures of land and gold.

The entries included here are all published books or pamphlets. Not included—because of the intention to limit this work to writings that are available to the general public, and also because of the attempt to keep this at a portable, practical size—are all unpublished manuscripts, all magazines and magazine articles, newspaper articles, obvious fiction, all biographies of a third-person nature, and (with a few exceptions) all state and county historical publications that utilize a multiple interest format.

Introduction

A trail: to many of us it has the power to produce mystery, curiosity, and even romance. It can create a wonder that elicits much more than just interest in a worn path leading from one place to another. To stand in its well-worn furrow and cast an eye to the fading traces as it crosses the horizon can immediately fill the mind with a number of vexing questions: How long has it been there? Who made it? Where does it go?

If you believe as some do, that inquisitiveness is an unchanging facet of human nature, then you can better perceive the magnetism that the longest of all trails must have had during the first half of the nineteenth century on the many thousands of visionaries looking west—west along the long trail to Oregon.

In those years the Oregon Territory was little more than a name; an enigma lying on the distant slope of the far-off Rocky Mountains. Between the limits of the frontier and these mountains (mountains which few had ever seen, not to mention crossed) ranged the unpopulated plains, called by many "The Great American Desert." To most Americans, especially a wife happily settled among friends and relatives, it seemed like a very long way to travel. And she was right! It was a staggering distance to travel considering the unseen destination and the only road to it, at best, uncertain. Knowledge concerning Oregon, and the trail to it, came mostly from a smattering of readings[1] or from the hearsay liberally disseminated at every meeting place from the local ale house corner table to the more rural, corner fence post.

The foremost news source of the day, newspapers, were responsible for many of the colorful rumors and most of the limited information

---

1. See for example, *The Rocky Mountains: Or Adventures in the Far West* by Washington Irving, first printed in 1837. Or, Irving's *Astoria*, printed in 1836.

pertaining to the trail west. As early as March 11, 1926, the *Missouri Advocate and St. Louis Enquirer* had published the startling news, "New Route to the Pacific Ocean, discovered by Genl. (sic) William H. Ashley, during his late Expedition to the Rocky Mountains" in which it is stated, concerning the route between St. Louis and the Pacific Ocean, ". . . that thousands may travel it in safety, without meeting any obstruction deserving the name of a Mountain."[2] Those having access to this paper (and the ability to read it) would have noted this significant statement by a well respected and experienced explorer. Others would learn of what Ashley said via second-hand or third-hand conversations which very likely had been exaggerated to varying degrees. Just a year later, in 1827, Ashley in an exploit related to the fur trade, wheeled a cannon all the way to the Great Salt Lake;[3] the first wheeled vehicle to be taken so far west.

Just three years later, three of history's most famous members of the fur trade, Jed Smith, William Sublette, and David Jackson, hee-hawed ten wagons tugged by four mules each, plus two dearborns each pulled by a mule, and eighty-one riders, all on mules, from St. Louis to the rendezvous at Wind River in what is now Wyoming.[4] And in 1832, Captain Benjamin Bonneville, later to be the subject of Washington Irving's book on the Rocky Mountains, would cause even a greater degree of speculation by proving it was possible to pass over the Continental Divide with wagons.

In the mid-thirties a monumental event took place. Until this time the only penetration of the remote mountain regions had been by the rugged members of the fur trade, or by hardy explorers or adventurers. But now two missionaries, Marcus Whitman and Henry Spaulding, determined to travel west, decided they would attempt it with wagons. The wagons got as far as they did probably because the missionary party was fortunate enough, upon starting overland, to become a part of the American Fur Company's assemblage headed for a Rocky Mountain rendezvous. The impact of the missionary party as it disappeared over the horizon was not lost on those who had been considering the venture, for Whitman and Spaulding had taken their eastern-bred wives, Narcissa and Eliza, with them.

It seems quite probable that the average frontier landowner may

2. *The West of William H. Ashley.* Dale L. Morgan, ed., Denver, 1964, p. 140.
3. Ibid., p. 166.
4. *The Great Platte River Road.* Merrill J. Mattes, Nebraska State Historical Society, 1969, p. 12.

have concluded, upon hearing this development, that if those tender-tendoned, parlour pansies (or words to that effect) from the east could make the trip to Oregon, then his Sarah-Belle, accustomed to the rigors of pioneer life, should certainly have no trouble. During the later part of the decade, with the continued outfittings of fur traders, large caravans bound for Santa Fe, and news of other travelers, such as the hunter, Sir William Drummond Stewart,[5] it became impossible for the rousing trails to the west to be anything but a continued red-hot subject for the newspapers and a principal topic of discussion among the gentry.

And so, it is no wonder when 1840 arrived, the question of heading for Oregon arrived with it. The arguments, pro and con, would be recounted many times through the next decade. Newspapers all over the country had their say. Even British papers, because the northern boundary of the Oregon Territory was still in question (and would be until 1846), joined the fanfare with their two-pence worth.

In his exhaustive book on overland travel, *The Plains Across*,[6] John D. Unruh discusses in the chapter "Public Opinion 1840–42" the array of arguments brought forth as to whether the trek west would be "palpable homicide" or "merry as a marriage bell." He deduces that much of one's opinion, concerning the venture, had to be derived from the sources one had access to. Unruh concludes, "In view of the prevailing climate of opinion in their locality, it doubtless took much courage for some to set out. . . ."[7]

But set out they did! In 1840, Joel Walker, his family, and three missionary couples journeyed to Oregon under the auspices of the American Fur Company. The next year, 1841, the former trapper, Thomas "Broken Hand" Fitzpatrick, would lead the first emigrant train, the Bidwell-Bartleson party, as far as Soda Springs, near Fort Hall, in what is now southeast Idaho, before leaving the Bidwell group to persevere by its own means to California. Thirty-four resolute souls struggled on to California; twenty-four from the same train took the road to Oregon. In 1842, one hundred and forty-two emigrants traveled to Oregon.[8] The greatest mass emigration this country would experience had begun.

5. See *Prairie and Mountain Sketches*, Matthew C. Field, edited by Kate L. Gregg and John Francis McDermott, 1957, University of Oklahoma.
6. 1979, University of Illinois, p. 28–61.
7. Ibid., p. 61.
8. Ibid., p. 119.

If the trail west was hazardous, the exact destination unsure, and the benefits argumentable, what determining factor would provide the motivation for such a proposition of chance? Possibly there were as many reasons to go west as there were emigrants going. According to Aubrey L. Haines in his book *Historic Sites Along the Oregon Trail:* "There was a profit motive behind the initial development, but its use was later dictated by religious fervor, rampart nationalism, and, most important, the common man's restlessness—his desire to escape from frontier poverty, the debilitating illnesses then prevalent in the Mississippi Valley, and his all-too-familiar neighbors."[9] Added to this perceptive list, although certainly not applicable to all emigrants, should be the insidious quality of greed. Certainly during the rush to the gold fields of California, and on a lesser scale to the later discoveries of ore in Idaho and nowaday Montana, greed must be listed as the number one motivating factor.

But whatever the reason weighing the decision of a future emigrant in favor of giving up his home and friends for a speculative future, once his decision to go west was made that might be all that was needed to tip the scales for a like conclusion from a watchful neighbor who had, up to that moment, been unable to make up his mind. And neighbor was sure to tell neighbor, while casting a thoughtful eye westward, that his neighbor's neighbor had left for Oregon. Excitement: it's a great salesman!

Figures taken from the newspapers of the day, emigrant registers, military reports and less factual sources such as the overland journals, appear to set the number of emigrants between 1840 and 1865 as somewhere around 300,000. The study, *The Plains Across*, supplies a similar figure for the period 1840 to 1860.[10] *The Great Platte River Road* contains an estimate of 350,000 through 1866.[11] Some other, less scholarly efforts, give totals as high as 500,000.

Whichever figure is used, it seems amazing that so many, of all ages, perceived the epic bounds of this massive experience and resolved to leave a written record of their participation. Even the most impoverished imagination was supplied with an endless variety of subject matter to choose from: the trail, wagon problems, landmarks, stifling dust, mosquitoes, wild buffalo, the endless line of graves and dead

9. 1981, Patrice Press, Gerald, Mo., p. 5.

10. *The Plains Across*, John D. Unruh, Jr., University of Illinois, 1979, p. 120.

11. *The Great Platte River Road.* Merrill J. Mattes, Nebraska State Historical Society, 1969, p. 5.

animals, and the debilitating consequences of the journey itself. Some wrote marveling at the opposite result: an individual of weak constitution finding himself attaining a vastly more robust nature as the days passed.

There were very few, however, that found the experience physically helpful. To most, surrounded by danger—imagined or real—and death, chilling in its quickness and cruelty, it was a time to question their own sanity in deciding to undertake such a folly. The journals tell their stories: the deaths, the dangers, the drama, and the resulting excitement of an event in American history that has no counterpart.

The scenario for this mighty emigration westward reads like an exaggerated Hollywood script: an unknown trail through two thousand miles of unmapped (or at best uncertain) country, wild Indians, sickness and death, deep dangerous rivers, incredible mountains, and vast deserts. And yet it was all there, to be assimilated, step-by-step, by each enterprising member journeying to a new home. It is no wonder so many of those who survived (and the vast majority did) were moved to leave some lasting record of their role in this unique moment of history.

This book is an attempt to gather together, for the first time, all published accounts by those who were involved in the overland story, and were, for varying reasons taking the Oregon Trail westward during the years 1841 to 1864. Included are contemporary diaries, many of which were written along the trail. Other entries were set down in an author's fading years. It does not seem surprising that many of the reminiscences refer to this interlude as the highlight of a lifetime.

The writers of this book were the young; the old; the physically weak; the morally strong; the healthy; and even the deaf. It was you, and it was me, one hundred and fifty years ago.

Sources Consulted

(Bancroft)	The Bancroft Library. *University of California Catalog of Printed Books.* 22 vols. and supplements. Boston, 1964.
(Bradley)	Bradley, Van Allen. *The Book Collectors Handbook of Values.* 1982–83 ed., New York, 1982.
(Cowan)	Cowan, Robert E. and Robert G. *A Bibliography of the History of California and the Pacific Coast.* Los Angeles, 1964.

(Decker)   *Peter Decker's Catalogues of Americana* in Three Volumes including Index. Austin, 1979.

(Eberstadt)   Eberstadt, Edward. *Catalogs of Americana.* 4 vols. New York, 1965.

(Denver Library)   *Catalog of the Western History Department.* Boston, 1970.

(Mormons)   Bitton, Davis. *Guide to Mormon Diaries & Autobiographies.* Provo, Utah, 1977.

(New York Library) *Dictionary Catalog of the History of the Americas.* The New York Public Library Reference Department. Boston, 1961.

(Rittenhouse)   Rittenhouse, Jack D. *The Santa Fe Trail,* A Historic Bibliography. Albuquerque: University of New Mexico Press, 1971.

(Smith)   Smith, Charles W. *Pacific Northwest Americana.* Third ed. Revised and extended by Isabel Mayhew. Portland, 1950.

(Soliday)   *The George W. Soliday Collection of Western Americana.* Compiled by Peter Decker. New York, 1960.

(Streeter)   *The Celebrated Collection of Americana formed by the Late Thomas Winthrop Streeter.* 7 Vols. New York, 1966.

(Yale Library)   *Catalog of the Yale Collection of Western Americana.* 4 Vols. Boston, n.d.

Illustrations

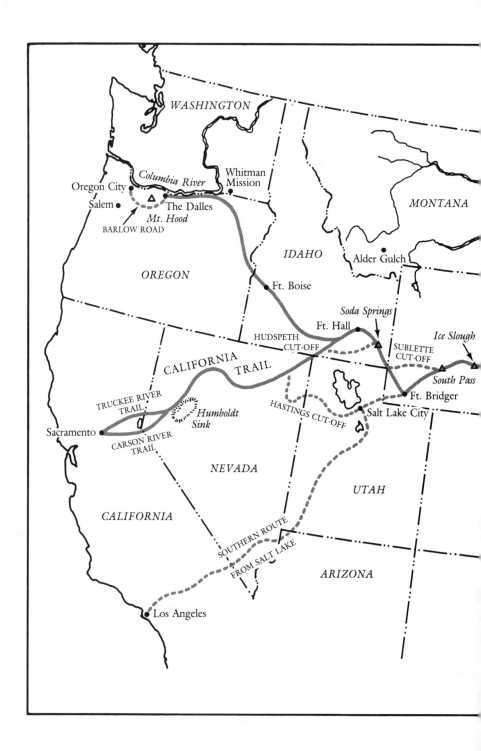

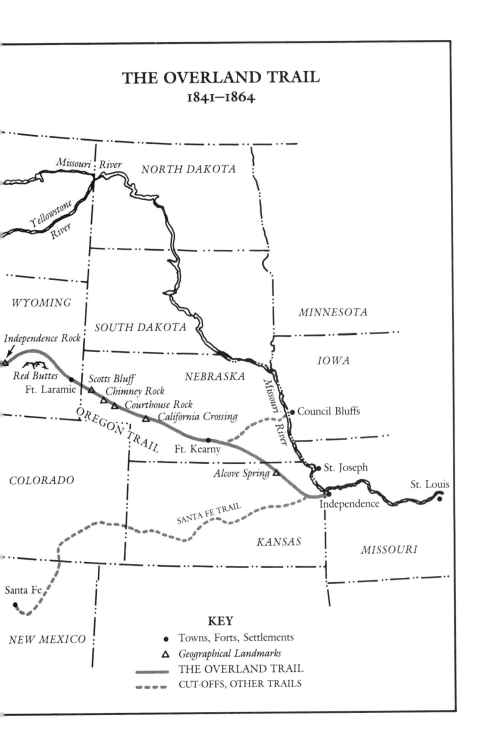

THE OVERLAND TRAIL
1841–1864

KEY
- ● Towns, Forts, Settlements
- △ *Geographical Landmarks*
- ▬▬ THE OVERLAND TRAIL
- ---- CUT-OFFS, OTHER TRAILS

JOURNAL OF TRAVELS

OVER THE

ROCKY MOUNTAINS,

TO THE

MOUTH OF THE COLUMBIA RIVER;

MADE DURING THE YEARS 1845 AND 1846:

CONTAINING MINUTE DESCRIPTIONS OF THE

VALLEYS OF THE WILLAMETTE, UMPQUA, AND CLAMET;

A GENERAL DESCRIPTION OF

OREGON TERRITORY;

ITS INHABITANTS, CLIMATE, SOIL, PRODUCTIONS, ETC., ETC.;

A LIST OF

NECESSARY OUTFITS FOR EMIGRANTS;

AND A

Table of Distances from Camp to Camp on the Route.

ALSO;

A Letter from the Rev. H. H. Spalding, resident Missionary, for the last ten years, among the Nez Percé Tribe of Indians, on the Koos-koos-kee River; The Organic Laws of Oregon Territory; Tables of about 300 words of the Chinook Jargon, and about 200 Words of the Nez Percé Language; a Description of Mount Hood; Incidents of Travel, &c., &c.

BY JOEL PALMER.

CINCINNATI:
J. A. & U. P. JAMES, WALNUT STREET,
BETWEEN FOURTH AND FIFTH.
1847.

The best overland narrative for the year of 1845.

An engraving of Scott's Bluff by Frederick Piercy.

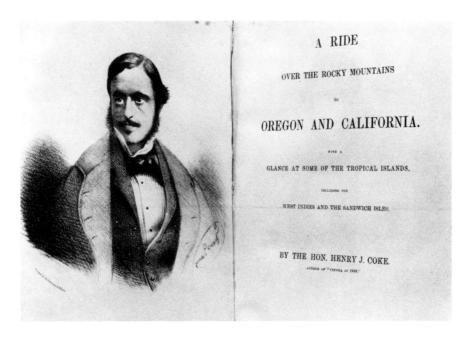

An entertaining narrative of 1850 and one of the West's best
adventure stories.

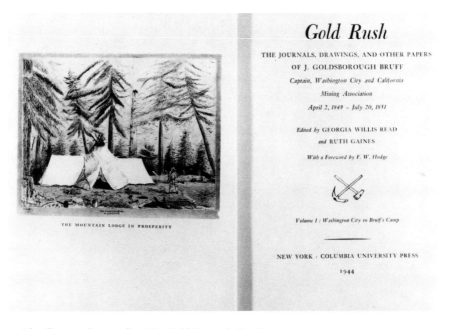

The illustrated journals of J. Goldsborough Bruff.

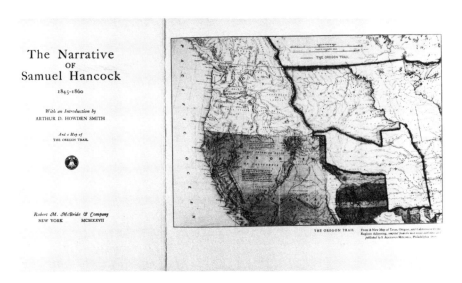

Samuel Hancock's 1845 narrative includes a firsthand account
of Meek's "Lost Wagon Train."

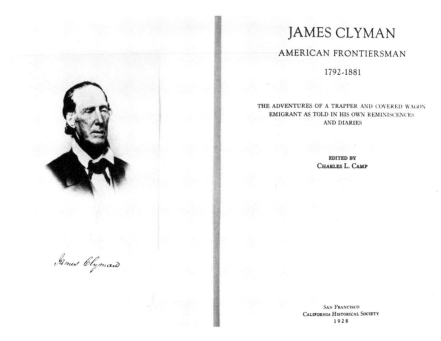

The Clyman journal is the only overland journal to Oregon for
the year 1844.

Taken from Fremont's narrative of 1842–1843—a classic of Western literature.

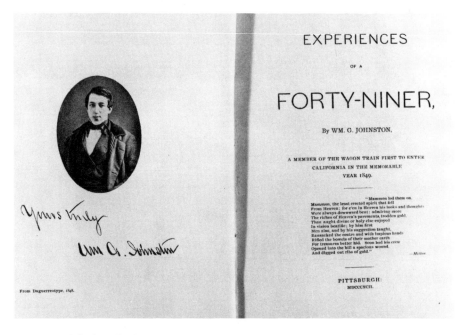

One of the best forty-niner narratives.

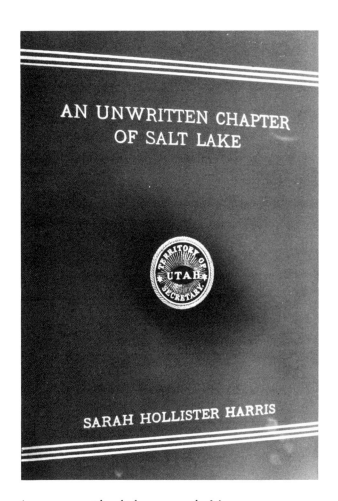

AN UNWRITTEN CHAPTER
OF SALT LAKE

SARAH HOLLISTER HARRIS

A very scarce title which concerns the Mormon movement.

The Trail:

A Bibliography

Regarding the entries

1. The date in brackets before the author's name indicates the year of travel by the participant.

2. In each entry to the right of the author's name is a code letter (conveniently similar, it is hoped, to the system used by Wright Howes in his bibliography *U.S.iana*) which represents the current value of the entry. The price range for each has been carefully derived from auction records, published price guides, and booksellers' catalogs. Generally speaking, the scarcer a desired item, the higher its value. There are twelve classifications as follows:

a —	up to $50	c —	$350 to 500
aa —	50 to 100	cc —	500 to 750
aaa —	100 to 150	ccc —	750 to 1000
b —	150 to 200	d —	1000 to 2000
bb —	200 to 250	dd —	2000 to 5000
bbb —	250 to 350	ddd —	5000 and over

3. Names in parentheses refer to those who edited or recorded a first-hand account of a trip made by someone other than himself.

4. Much of the binding, design, and printing of the books included in this bibliography has been expertly and attractively done by notable printers. This enhances the books to the appreciative collector, if not the average reader, and is generally mentioned where applicable.

5. Each entry includes a further bibliographic reference list the reader may consult for additional information. These references were selected, after much consideration, on their compatibility with the subject, and their relative availability to the public, book dealers, and collectors. The books, and the abbreviations used for them, are as follows:

C   Cowan. Robert E. and Robert G. *A Bibliography of the History of the Pacific Coast 1510–1930.* Los Angeles, 1964. New ed.

E   Edwards. E. I. *Desert Voices. A Descriptive Bibliography.* Los Angeles, 1958.

G   Graff. Everett D. *A Catalogue of the Collection of Everett D. Graff Collection of Western America.* Compiled by Colton Storm, Chicago: University of Chicago, 1968.

H   Howes. Wright. *USiana.* New York, 1962. (rev. & enlarged ed.)

P   Paher. Stanley W. *An Annotated Bibliography.* Las Vegas, 1980.

W   Wheat. Carl. *Books of the Gold Rush.* San Francisco (1949).

WC   Wagner-Camp-Becker. *The Plains and the Rockies.* San Francisco: John Howell-Books (fourth ed.), 1982.

Z   *Zamorano 80.* Los Angeles, 1945.

Much detective work is necessary in a project such as this. Darkened corners are lit, musty records and films are perused, errant clues are followed till they pinch out, and numerous dead ends are reached. A number of these false leads are listed under the heading of "Red Herrings," in hopes of shortening the path for future travelers. Information regarding those who traveled a southern trace across this country is more meaty, while the listings for those who opted for a water route to reach the western coast are, because of the difference in modus operandi, quite brief.

I have rechecked every entry repeatedly in an attempt to keep mistakes at a minimum. I hope I have been successful.

Abbreviations

ad., ads.	advertisement
anr.	another
cm, cms	centimeter(s)
co.	company(s)
ed(s).	edition(s), editor(s)
e-map	map on endpapers
facs.	facsimile
f-map	folded map
frontis	frontispiece
H.R.	House of Representatives
illus.	illustrations
impr.	imprint
n. d.	no date
n. p.	no place
p., pp.	page(s)
port.	portrait
pvt. ptd, ptg.	privately printed, printing
rev.	revised
rpt.	reprint
Sen.	Senate
S.F.	San Francisco
SLC	Salt Lake City
wraps	bound in wrappers

1. [1850] **Abbey, James**   ddd
    *California, A Trip Across the Plains, in the Spring of 1850, Being
    a Daily Record of Incidents of the Trip Over the Plains, the Desert,
    and the Mountains, Sketches of the Country, Distances from Camp
    to Camp* . . . New Albany, Ind.: Kent & Norman and J.R.
    Nunemacher, 1850.
    pp. 64.

    Abbey traveled from St. Louis to Weaversville, California. Graff says,
    "The first parts of the work appeared during May, June, and July 1850,
    as a series of letters in the *New Albany Ledger*. It is the day-by-day
    account written by a young man who enjoyed his experiences." The
    Parke-Bernet Galleries in New York sold the only perfect copy in 1941.
    Ref.: C-p. 1, G-1, H-A5, WC-178

2. [1850] **Abbott, Carlisle S.**   aaa
    Recollections of a California Pioneer. New York: Neal Publishing
    Co., 1917.
    pp. 235, frontis

    Abbott was a member of the Beloit Company. He tells of his trip to
    the gold mines in 1850 and of some of his experiences there.
    Ref.: C-p. 1, G-2, W-1

3. [1852] **Ackley, Mary E.**   bb
    *Crossing the Plains and Early Days in California: Memories of
    Girlhood Days in California's Golden Age.* San Francisco: pvt.
    ptg., 1928.
    pp. 68, 7 plates (including frontis)

    A scarce book on overland travel. Mary Ackley's party traveled from
    Clark County, Missouri, to Sacramento in five months.
    Ref.: C-p. 2, H-A33

4. [1852] **Adams, David Maddux**   a
    *Biographical Sketch, Including an Account of Crossing the Plains
    in 1852.* Chicago and New York: Lewis Publishing, 1912.
    pp. 12

    Reprinted from *American Biography and Geneaology* (Vol. 2); California
    edition, edited by R. J. Burnette, 1912. Notes by the author's son,
    Douglas S. Adams, are on the last page.
    Ref.: none

5. [1850] **Adams, Elias** aa
   Ancestors and Descendants of Elias Adams the Pioneer . . . Edited by Frank D. Adams, Kaysville, Utah: pvt. ptg., 1929.
   pp. 260

Adams relates the trip he took over the plains as a Mormon pioneer. One chapter is devoted to the Donner story.
   Ref.: none

6. [1848] **Adams, W. L.** bbb
   Lecture on the Oregon and the Pacific Coast. Boston, 1869.
   pp. 39

A very rare book. A little known account of an early Oregon pioneer who gives a description of his journey from Illinois to Oregon in 1848.
   Ref.: none

7. [1852] **Akin, James** b
   Journal of James Akin, Jr. Edited by Edward Everett Dale, Norman: University of Oklahoma Press, 1919.
   pp. 32, map, facs.

This is Bulletin No. 172, University Studies No. 9, of which only a few copies appear to exist outside of the country's libraries. It tells the story of an ox team trip during which seven people died. Akin was eighteen at the time and kept a daily record of the trip from Iowa to the Dalles, in Oregon. The Howes reference to 1842 is probably a misprint.
   Ref.: G-27, H-A95

8. [1842] **Allen, A. J.** bbb
   Ten Years in Oregon: Travels and Adventures of Doctor E. White and Lady. Ithaca: Mack, Andrus and Co., 1842.
   pp. 399, map, frontis of Dr. and Mrs. White (Allen)
   rpt.: another ed. omitted the port. and had 430 pages. Pages 399–430 have to do with the Fremont narrative. Other eds. appeared in 1850 (different title) and 1859 in New York.

They started from Independence in May of 1842, in company with Medorem Crawford with L. W. Hastings joining later. Allen speaks of obtaining Thomas Fitzpatrick as guide at Ft. Laramie to take them to Ft. Hall.
   Ref.: G-36, H-A131, WC-144

9. [1852] **(Allen, Eleanor)** a
Canvas Caravans. Based on the Journal of Esther Belle McMillan Hanna, who . . . brought the Presbyterian Colony to Oregon in 1852. Portland, 1946.
pp. 134

Esther and her husband, Rev. Joseph Hanna, made their journey motivated by the desire to establish a new base for their religion in the Northwest.
Ref.: none

10. [1843] **Applegate, Jesse** ccc
Recollections of My Boyhood. Roseburg, Oreg.: Review Publishing, 1914.
pp. 99, wraps

"One of the great overland narratives, and the classic account of the Oregon migration of 1843. He traveled, as a nine-year-old boy, with his family from Missouri to Oregon, where they settled in the Willamette Valley, becoming prosperous and influential pioneers in the Territory. His reminiscences provided an interesting, detailed, and perceptive record of the crossing and the first decade of life in the Oregon country, which was still a dangerous and hostile environment for the frontiersman."—John Howell Books
This book is by the son of Jesse Applegate, Sr. who wrote his own version of the trek in "A Day with the Cow Column in 1843."
Ref.: G-75, H-A294

11. [1843] **Applegate, Jesse Sr.** aaa
A Day with the Cow Column in 1843. Chicago: Caxton Club, 1934.
pp. 207 300 copies
rpt.: 1952, Portland.

Also includes his son Jesse's, "Recollections of My Boyhood." Jesse Sr. was famous as the originator of the Applegate Trail into Oregon.
Ref.: G-74, H-A294

12. [1846] **Aram, Joseph** cc
In Memory of Joseph Aram. San Jose: (circa 1898)
pp. 24 (unnumbered), frontis, port., wraps

Contains a five page "Memory" by Mrs. G. C. Aram along with two pages of "Tributes" by Revs. M. C. Briggs and F. F. Jewell. The rest of the book is "Early Reminiscences written for a Pioneer" by Aram. He tells of leaving Illinois with his family in 1846 to emigrate to California. A copy of this book sold in the late Sixties at the Streeter auction for $375.00.
Ref.: none

13.   [1864] **Argyle, Archie**   b
           Cupid's Album. New York: M. Doolady, 1866.
           pp. 332
Argyle traveled with the train of Capt. Armath out of St. Joseph. He
tells of camp differences and the difficulties of the trail. Howes states
that the author's real name was Annie Argyle. The book is a fictionalized version of actual experiences.
           Ref.: none

14.   [1849] **Arms, Cephas**   a
           *The Long Road to California. The Journal of Cephas Arms Sup-
           plemented with Letters by Traveling Companions on the Overland
           Trail in 1849.* Mount Pleasant, Mich.: Private Press of John
           Cumming (1985).
           pp. 142, frontis, illus.   487 copies ptd.
Arms was a Lieutenant in the Knox County Company of Illinois. His
company joined a larger train, part of which became famous as the
Jayhawkers of Death Valley fame. Arms was one of the party that was
lured away from the main route by those touting a shortcut to California. However, he and the few members of the company who had
followed him, were soon forced to turn back by the impassibility of a
vast canyon. This irony shortened his trip and may have saved his
life. The Jayhawkers party, not burdened with wagons, continued on
foot to the miseries of Death Valley. (*See* Asa Haynes [Ellenbecker,
141]; 193–95; 325.) A nicely printed book.
           Ref.: none

15.   [1852] **Bagley, Clarence B.**   aaa
           The Acquisition and Pioneering of Old Oregon. Seattle: Argus
           Printing, 1924.
           pp. 41, frontis, 4 plates, 16 ports., wraps
Bagley traveled with the Bethel Company. He tells of the trip, of early
Oregon, and of the founding of Seattle.
           Ref.: none

16.   [1853] **Bailey, Washington**   c
           *A Trip to California in 1853 . . . Recollections of a Gold Seeking
           Trip by Ox Train across the Plains and Mountains by an Old
           Illinois Pioneer.* Leroy, Ill.: Leroy Journal, 1915.
           pp. 50, port., wraps, errata slip after p. 46
Bailey made the trip from Indiana with a party headed by his uncle,
Joshua. They took with them 1500 sheep and 500 cattle. This large
assemblage crossed the Sierra Mountains at the Carson River head-
waters.
           Ref.: C-p. 28, G-139, H-B35

17. [1853]   **Baker, George Holbrook**   b
    Crossing the Plains. Views Drawn from Nature in 1853 . . .
    Sacramento, 1853.
    1 leaf
Consists of thirteen scenes printed on one leaf folded once.
    Ref.: none

18. [1859]   **Baker, Hozial H.**   dd, rpt.: aa
    Overland Journey to Carson Valley, Utah; Through Kansas, Ne-
    braska, and Utah; also, Return Trip from San Francisco to Seneca
    Falls, via the Isthmus. Seneca Falls, N.Y.: Published by F.M.
    Baker, 1861.
    pp. 38, port., illus. (7), wraps
    rpt.: *Overland Journey to Carson Valley & California.* San Fran-
       cisco, pp. 91
Baker was a seventy-year-old man at the time he went over the trail.
After surviving the strenuous Humboldt route, he almost died while
attempting to walk from Genoa over the Sierras by himself. Beautifully
reprinted by the Book Club of California. Of the first edition, four
copies are known to exist.
    Ref.: G-142, H-B49, WC-367a

19. [1850]   **Baldwin, J. F.**   aaa
    Diary Kept by J. F. Baldwin while Crossing the Plains in 1850.
    San Francisco: California Patron & Agriculturist Printers,
    1887.
    pp. 15
This short account is quite rare.
    Ref.: none

20. [1849]   **Ball, Nicholas**   aaa
    The Pioneers of '49: A History of the Excursion of the Society of
    California Pioneers of New England from Boston to the Leading
    Cities of the Golden State April 10–May 17, 1890. Boston,
    1891.
    pp. 288, illus.
Ball originally went over the plains as a forty-niner. This journey is
told as a then-and-now comparison, including many poignant comments about the changes which had taken place over the intervening
years.
    Ref.: H-B67, W-9

21. [1857] **Bandel, Eugene**   aa
     Frontier Life in the Army, 1854–1861. Edited by Ralph P.
     Bieber. Translated by Olga Bandel and Richard Jente. Glen-
     dale: Arthur H. Clark Co., 1932.
     pp. 330, frontis, illus.

Bandel, a member of the Army, tells of traveling to Utah and from
there following the Humboldt to California. He talks of Colonel Albert
Sidney Johnston, General William Harney, and of the Mormon unrest.
Bandel's story is taken from his journal, kept in English, and his letters,
which were in German. This is the second publication in the Southwest Historical Series.
     Ref.: none

22. [1859] **Barnett, Joel**   aa
     A Long Trip in a Prairie Schooner. Whittier, Calif.: Western
     Stationery, 1928.
     pp. 134, 2 ports.   350 copies

Barnett wrote this account based on the diary left by John Millican,
a member of the party, and one of a number of that group who died
almost immediately after reaching Oregon. Parts of this little book do
a good job of communicating the varied feelings of those on the trail;
other sections are most certainly fictionalized. The elder Barnetts, who
are pictured in the two included ports., stayed in Oregon seven years
before returning to Iowa.
     Ref.: G-191

23. [1850] **(Barrows, William)**   aa
     *The General; or Twelve Nights in the Hunter's Camp. A Narrative
     of Real Life.* Boston: Lee and Shepard, 1869.
     pp. 268, frontis, plates
     rpt.: 1870, Boston

This is a biography by William of his brother, General Willard Barrows.
It includes some information concerning the General's trip over the
plains to California in 1850 and of his later trips to Montana and
Idaho.
     Ref.: C-p. 830, G-196, H-B188

24. [1852] **Barton, William Kilshaw**   a
     *Copy of Diary and Missionary Journal of William Kilshaw Barton,
     Pioneer of 1852.* Salt Lake City, 1966.
     pp. 38

Barton crossed the plains to reach Utah in 1852. He gives a brisk
outline of his life.
     Ref.: none

25. [1860] **Batty, Joseph**   c
Over the Wilds to California; or Eight Years from Home. Edited
by Rev. John Simpson. Leeds, Eng.: J. Parrott, 1867.
pp. 64

This appears to be an account of an overland trip in 1860. The exact
year is difficult to pinpoint as Batty writes without specific references
to dates and places. Moving to Wisconsin in 1858 or 1859, he stayed
only a short time with his brother's family before unsuccessfully trying
mining and farming in California.
Ref.: G-209, H-B240

26. [1845] **Bayley, Betsey**   a
Covered Wagon Women. Edited by Kenneth L. Holmes. Glen-
dale: Arthur H. Clark Co., 1983.
pp. 272, frontis, f-map, errata slip

Betsey's short letter occupies only a few pages of Volume I of this
valuable ten part series concerned with contemporary diaries and letters of women traveling overland. Heading for Oregon, she was a
member of the party led by Stephen Meek.
Ref.: none

27. [1847] **Bean, George Washington**   a
*Autobiography of George Washington Bean, a Utah Pioneer of
1847 and His Family Records.* Compiled by Flora Diana Bean
Horne. Salt Lake City: Flora D. B. Horne, (1945).
pp. 259

Bean was an early emigrant to the Salt Lake area, and here tells some
of his experiences traveling there. He also relates the well known story
of the crickets and seagulls.
Ref.: none

28. [1853] **Beeson, John**   cc
*A Plea for the Indians; with Facts and Features of the Late War
in Oregon.* New York: Published by John Beeson, 1857.
pp. 143 and 1 (ads), wraps

Beeson left Illinois in March and traveled by way of the Humboldt to
the Rogue River, arriving at the end of September. The second edition
carries the same imprint, date, and collation.
Ref.: G-233, H-B314, WC-284

29.   [1841]   **Belden, Josiah**   a
             *Josiah Belden: 1841 California Overland Pioneer: His Memoir
             and His Early Letters.* Edited by Doyce B. Nunis, Jr. George-
             town: Talisman Press, 1962.
             pp. 150, map, illus.   750 copies
A member of the Bidwell-Bartleson party, his memoir supplies another
view of the first planned overland journey to California for the purpose
of settling.
             Ref.: P-111

30.   [1848]   **Belknap, Keturah**   a
             Covered Wagon Women. Edited by Kenneth L. Holmes. Glen-
             dale: Arthur H. Clark Co., 1983.
             pp. 272, frontis, f-map, errata slip
The high spot of this first volume of the ten volume series is the
wonderful account of early pioneer life as told by Keturah Belknap.
Her singular style of writing includes the interesting preparations for
the trip to Oregon, along with incidences of the journey itself. Sadly,
her duties precluded the finishing of her diary, and her reporting comes
to an end near Ft. Hall.
             Ref.: none

31.   [1853]   **Belshaw, George**   a
             1853 Diary of the Oregon Trail. Eugene, Oreg.: Lane County
             Pioneer Historical Society, 1960.
             pp. 52, port., heavy wraps
Belshaw journeyed from Iowa to the Willamette Valley as captain of
a ten-wagon party. The somewhat dry narrative is made more colorful
by Belshaw's original spelling, which has been left unchanged. Another Lane County publication bound in heavy wraps and printed on
the rectos only.
             Ref.: none

32.   [1860]   **Bemis, Stephen A.**   aaa
             Recollections of a Long and Somewhat Uneventful Life. St. Louis:
             pvt. ptg., 1932.
             pp. 92, port.
The "recollections" concern for the most part his attempts to become
a success in business, and include sailing to the mines in 1852, opening
a restaurant in San Francisco, and selling candles. Also included is a
brief description of a second trip to California, this time overland.
             Ref.: none

33. [1850] **Bennett, James**   aa
        *Overland Journey to California. Journal of James Bennett Whose
        Party left New Harmony in 1850 and Crossed the Plains and
        Mountains until the Golden West Was Reached.* New Harmony,
        Ind.: Times Print, 1906.
        (New York: Eberstadt, 1932.) Has above imprint on cover.
        pp. 45, wraps   200 copies
A colorful report written by a journalist, this was first printed serially
in the *New Harmony Times.* Bennett speaks ominously and often, of
the illness and death along the trail. He also gives a good account of
the suffering encountered by those following the Humboldt, and of
the many dead animals, stating that in the first five miles he counted
the carcasses of sixty-four oxen and fifty-five horses.
        Ref.: C-p. 831, G-261, H-B357a

34. [1849] **Bidlack, Russell Eugene**   a
        Letters Home; The Story of Ann Arbor's Forty-niners. Ann Ar-
        bor: Ann Arbor Publishing, 1960.
        pp. 56, illus.
Includes extracts from the letters of local residents who wrote to those
still at home in Michigan, telling of their trip west and life in California.
        Ref.: none

35. [1841] **Bidwell, John**   aaa (1937 ed.)
        A Journey to California. St. Louis or Liberty, Mo., 1842 (?).
        pp. 32
        anr. ed.: 1937, S.F., pp. 48
A classic of its kind, depicting with grim realism the hazards and
frustrations experienced by the emigrants of the first wagon train to
California. Since the title page and wrapper are missing from the only
known copy (Bancroft Library), date and place of publication are
uncertain (see 1982 WC for discussion). In 1907 it was reprinted as
part of *Addresses, Reminiscences, etc., of General John Bidwell,* compiled
by C. C. Royce (Chico, Calif.). The latest reprint was done in 1964
(Berkeley: The Friends of the Bancroft Library). However, since the
first printing is virtually unobtainable, the beautifully printed 1937
edition by John Henry Nash is a worthy substitute.
        Ref.: C-p. 51, H-B433, WC-88

36. [1841] **Bidwell, John** aa
Echoes of the Past: An Account of the First Emigrant Train to California, Fremont and the Conquest of California, the Discovery of Gold and Early Reminiscences. Chico: Chico Advertiser, 1914.
pp. 94, wraps
Bidwell, along with Sutter, was identified with most early-day events around Sacramento.
Ref.: C-p. 52, G-292, H-B432, P-127, W-16

37. [1847] **Bingham, Erastus** aa
Sketch of the Life of Erastus Bingham and Family; Utah Pioneers of 1847. Compiled by Norman F. Bingham, Lillian B. Belnap, and Lester Scoville (Ogden, Utah, 1953).
pp. 68, illus.
Bingham was one of the early Utah emigrants. A folding chart referring to pedigrees is included.
Ref.: none

38. [1853] **(Bixby-Smith, Sarah)** aa
Adobe Days, Being the Truthful Narrative . . . with an Account of How Three Young Men from Maine in 1853 Drove Sheep and Cattle across the Plains, Mountains and Deserts from Illinois to the Pacific Coast. . . . Cedar Rapids: Torch Press, 1925.
pp. 208
2nd ed.: 1926, pp. 217
This concerns the journal of Llewellyn Bixby and has a short chapter telling of the drive of a large herd of animals over the plains on Bixby's return trip to California.
Ref.: C-p. 55

39. [1847] **Blanchet, A. M. A.** 1st: bbb, rpt.: a
Voyage de l'eveque de Walla-Walla. Quebec: De L'Imprimerie de Fréchette & Cie, 1851.
pp. 28
rpt.: "Journal of a Catholic Bishop on the Oregon Trail . . .", 1979, Fairfield, Wash.
Printed in *Rapport sur les missions du Diocese de Quebec*, March, 1851. Blanchet gives a brief account of traveling from Westport to Oregon. The reprint was translated from the original journal which has been held by the Seattle Archdiocese for over 100 years.
Ref.: WC-195

40. [1854] **Blood, Jane Wilkie H.** a
Jane Wilkie Hooper Blood, Autobiography and Abridged Diary.
Edited by Ivy Hooper Blood Hill. Logan, Utah: J. P. Smith,
1966.
pp. 141
A diary revolving around Mormon life. The author's daughter married
a gentile resulting in what the author called, "one of the miserable
days of my life."
Ref.: none

41. [1849] **(Blood, Katie E.)** bbb
Memories of a Forty-niner. New Haven: Associated Publishers
of American Records, 1907.
pp. 27, wraps (red)
The forty-niner was John E. Browne, the author's father. This is a
day-by-day journal of his trip from Tennessee to the mines in California. At the conclusion of the book he is off for the diggings.
Ref.: C-p. 58, H-B544 (see also B852)

42. [1845] **Bonney, Benjamin Franklin** a
*Across the Plains by Prairie Schooner: Personal Narrative of B.
F. Bonney of His Trip to Sutter's Fort, California in 1846.* Edited
by Fred Lockley. Eugene, Oreg.: pvt. ptg., n. d.
pp. 20, wraps
This is from an interview with the author who actually crossed the
plains in 1845. He mentions the trains of Joel Palmer, Samuel K.
Barlow, and Samuel Hancock, and speaks of his experiences as a
member of the party led by Barlow. Bonney tells how his father Jarvis
was the first to leave the Barlow train at Fort Hall to follow the guide
Caleb Greenwood to California. This also includes a version of the
story of the man named Kinney and his Indian "slave." Bonney's party
reached Oregon from Sutter's Fort.
Ref.: none

43. [1849] **Booth, Edmund** a
Edmund Booth, Forty-niner. Stockton: San Joaquin Pioneer
Historical Society, 1953.
pp. 72, frontis, 1 illus.
In these reminiscences of a deaf pioneer, the author included the
fragmentary diary of his journey to California. Originally written with
pencil, some pages of the diary were illegible, while other pages were
lost. The entries begin with Booth fifty miles west of Independence
Rock, in central Wyoming.
Ref.: none

44. [1853] **Booth, John**   b
     In Memorial: John Booth, born in York, England . . . 1818, Died
     in Austin, Nevada . . . 1884. Austin: Reese River Reveille,
     1884.
     wraps (pink)
     pp. 8
A rare pamphlet about a Nevada newspaperman, only 2 or 3 copies
are known to exist. He crossed the plains to California in 1853, settling
in Calavaras County. Before producing newspapers in such towns as
Gold Hill, Pioche, Carson City, and Belmont, he drove an overland
stage.
     Ref.: none

45. [1851] **Booth, William**
     Early Utah Pioneers. Levi Hammon and Polly Chapman Bybee.
     Compiled by Betsy R. H. Greenwell. Kaysville: Inland Print-
     ing Co., n. d.
     pp. 50
This is the journal of an 1851 crossing of the plains in which Hammon
was captain of his group. Booth was the official clerk of the party. No
record of sale for this book was available.
     Ref.: none

46. [1862] **Boquist, Mrs. Laura Brewster**   aa
     Crossing the Plains with Ox Teams in 1862. (Los Angeles,
     1930).
     pp. 32
Mrs. Boquist traveled along the Platte and through Salt Lake City,
and speaks of greatly mistrusting the Mormons there.
     Ref.: none

47. [1847] **Braly, John Hyde**   a
     Memory Pictures, an Autobiography. (Los Angeles: The Neuner
     Co., 1912).
     pp. 263, frontis, plates
Braly went overland in 1847, and settled later in the Santa Clara
Valley of California.
     Ref.: C-p. 69, G-390

48. [1850] **Branstetter, Peter L.**   aaa
     Life and Travels of Peter L. Branstetter. St. Joseph, Mo.: Messenger of the Peace Publishers, (1913).
     pp. 203, port.

Branstetter tells of going over the plains to the diggings in 1850, and of his experiences while searching for riches. Also included is information regarding his return trip to Missouri, again going overland.
     Ref.: G-391, H-B723

49. [1846] **Breen, Patrick**   a, rpt.: a
     Diary of Patrick Breen. One of the Donner Party. Edited by Frederick J. Teggert. Berkeley: Publication of the Academy of Pacific Coast History, 1910.
     pp. 16, wraps (brown)
     rpt.: 1946, Book Club of California. Edited by George F. Stewart. 300 copies.

First published in the *California Star* May 22, 1847. This is an indispensable item for those interested in the Donner story. This tersely written narrative poignantly relates the days of hardship, as they happened, through the eyes of one who was there.
     Ref.: G-396, P-1869

50. [1850] **Brinkerhuff, Dick**   aaa
     Life and Adventures of Dick Brinkerhuff, One of Custar's Oldest Pioneers and Well Known throughout Wood County . . . Published in the Custar News in 1915. Custar, Ohio, 1915.
     pp. 31, wraps

Brinkerhuff says he went to California in 1850, and returned to Ohio in 1855. He went west again in 1857, spending much of his life on the plains and in California.
     Ref.: G-403, H-B777

51. [1849] **Bristol, C. C.**   cc
     Bristol's Traveller's Guide . . . to which Is Added the Routes to California, Carefully Compiled from the Most Reliable Sources . . . Buffalo: Jewett, Thomas & Co., (1849).
     pp. 48

According to Wagner-Camp-Becker, an earlier edition (1848) did not include the California route. Bristol's "most reliable sources" advised taking the Lassen cutoff.
     Ref.: H-B786, WC-179a

52. [1862] **Bristol, Rev. Sherlock**   b, rpt.: aa
The Pioneer Preacher. New York: Fleming H. Revell Co., 1887.
pp. 330, port., illus.
anr. ed.: 1887, Chicago, (title slightly changed)
rpt.: 1898, Chicago and New York, pp. 336 (includes additional chapter)
Bristol traveled by way of the Isthmus to the diggings in 1849 or possibly 1850, as he tends to be somewhat vague about his dates. In 1851 he was in San Francisco, literally loaded with gold, and headed home. Many years passed, "ten or twelve" according to the author, spent mostly preaching in the backwoods of Wisconsin. In 1862 (date uncertain), he captained a train to Oregon, relating many self-glorifying experiences from along the way. He recorded a talk with one of the two survivors of the Van Zandt train.
Ref.: C-p. 72, G-404, H-(1954)B1210

53. [1849] **Brooks, E. W.**   b
Journal of a Forty-niner. London: The Curwen Press, 1967.
pp. 67   50 copies
This book is somewhat of a modern rarity. Brooks traveled from Lorain County, Ohio, to the Sacramento Valley via Salt Lake City and the Humboldt River.
Ref.: none

54. [1852] **Brooks, Elisha**   1st: bbb, 2nd: aaa
Elisha Brooks, Life Story of a Pioneer. (San Francisco): pvt. ptg., 1922.
pp. 61, 2 ports.
2nd: 1922, pp. 61, 2 ports., Harr Wagner Pub.
The second edition contains corrections by the author. Brooks wrote this for his grandchildren to show them how the emigrants crossed the plains. He describes the trip taken when he was eleven years-old and in the company of his mother, Eliza Anna Brooks. His father, whom they were going to meet, had gone overland in 1850.
Ref.: C-p. 74, G-412, H-B815

55. [1850] **Brown, Adam Mercer**   ddd
The Gold Region, and Scenes by the Way; Being the Journal of a Tour by the Overland Route and South Pass of the Rocky Mountains, across the Great Basin and through California. Allegheny, Pa.: Purviance & Co., 1851.
pp. 136, wraps (blue)
Highly detailed, this very rare guidebook apparently was not known to Howes, Graff, or Wagner-Camp-Becker. Brown gives information concerning his route, which went from St. Joseph through South Pass,

to Great Salt Lake, then along the Humboldt River to the Carson Valley. Besides his fine discourse on the trail, he also speaks in depth about the Mormons, and the gold miners.

Ref.: none

56. [1856] **Brown, J. Robert** dd

Journal of a Trip across the Plains of the U.S. from Missouri to California, in the Year 1856: Giving a Correct View of the Country, Anecdotes, Indian Stories, Mountianeer' (sic) Tales, Etc. by J. Robert Brown Columbus: Published for the Author, 1860.

pp. 119, wraps

The Library of Congress and Princeton Library have the only two copies of the first printing known to exist, although Yale Library also reportedly has a copy. Should a copy appear for sale, it may well secure a higher price than what is indicated above.

Ref.: C-p. 833, H-B842, WC-352

57. [1859] **Brown, James Berry** aa

Journal of a Journey across the Plains in 1859. Edited by George R. Stewart. San Francisco: Book Club of California, 1970.

pp. 72, illus., printer's note 450 copies

When about twenty-two, Brown got "Pike's Peak fever" and started overland with his brother Jesse. Heading instead toward the coast, he took the "new" Lander cutoff which, according to Lander, carried 13,000 emigrants in 1859. Brown speaks frequently of the dust and considered it the trip's big bugaboo and the emigrant's worst enemy. Once he reached California he spent very little time prospecting.

Ref.: none

58. [1857] **Brown, John** aa

Autobiography of Pioneer John Brown. Salt Lake City, 1941.

pp. 491, illus.

Brown was one of the many who took part in the Mormon migration to Utah in 1847. He continued his travels during his life in efforts to help others in emigrating to the Salt Lake Valley.

Ref.: none

59. [1849] **Brown, John E.** b

Memoirs of a Forty-niner. New Haven, 1907.

pp. 28

A day-by-day diary telling of the experiences of those in the wagon train headed for the California riches. One experience mentioned was the desertion of the Captain and two others after cholera struck the members of the train.

Ref.: C-p. 833, H-B852

60. [1845] **Brown, John Henry**   1st: cc, rpt.: aa
            *Reminiscences and Incidents of "The Early Days" of San Francisco
            . . . from 1845 to 1850.* San Francisco, 1886.
            pp. 106, frontis
            rpt.: Grabhorn Press Rare Americana Series, Vol. 10, 1933,
                San Francisco, pp. 138, map, illus.
    His tales include only a brief account of an overland journey in 1845
    in the same party as Samuel Hancock, led by the misguided Stephen
    Meek. Brown actually made his first journey overland in 1843 to
    California as a fur trader. He speaks sparingly of this adventure as
    well.
            Ref.: H-B853, W-23

61. [1849] **Brown, Joseph**   d
            Crossing the Plains in 1849. Marysville, Calif.: Upton Bros.
            and Delzelle, 1916.
            pp. 38, wraps
    Even though printed at a relatively late date, this item is one of the
    rarest overland narratives. Very few copies are known to exist as only
    a small number of copies were printed for the family.
            Ref.: C-p. 833

62. [1846] **Brown, Tabitha**   a
            Covered Wagon Women. Edited by Kenneth L. Holmes. Glen-
            dale: Arthur H. Clark Co., 1983.
            pp. 272, frontis, f-map, errata slip
    Tabitha's story runs from page 47 to 65 of Volume I of this series. Her
    first letter tells of the many hazards of those first traveling the Applegate
    trail to Oregon. This letter is enlightening and informative. The sec-
    ond letter gives illustrations of later life in the area around Salem.
            Ref.: none

63. [1853] **Brown, William Richard**   a
            An Authentic Wagon Train Journal of 1853. Edited by Barbara
            Wills. Mokelumne Hill, Calif.: Horseshoe Printing (1985).
            pp. 79, illus., wraps with plastic perforated spine
    This is the day-by-day diary of William Richard Brown, grandfather
    of the editor. Wills notes the diary has been "interpreted and typed
    as accurately as possible from the handwritten original journals." Two
    pages of the journal are reproduced following pp. 79. Brown traveled
    the north side of the Platte, through Salt Lake City, and along the

Humboldt where, among his comments, he writes a glowing report of
the grass available for the livestock. He also mentions several heated
run-ins with other emigrants along the road.

Ref.: none

64.　[1849]　**Bruff, J. Goldsborough**　　　1st: bbb, anr. ed: aa
*Gold Rush: The Journals, Drawings, and Other Papers of J.
Goldsborough Bruff . . . April 2, 1849–July 20, 1851.* 2 vols.
Edited by Georgia Willis Read and Ruth Gaines. New York:
Columbia University Press, 1944.
pp. 1404, 2 frontis (1 colored), 98 plates, 3 f-maps
anr. ed.: 1949, New York, one vol. (abridged)

One of the most comprehensive and informative gold rush sources
available, not only for its picture of life in the diggings, but for its
highly detailed narrative, including Bruff's own sketches and drawings
of the overland crossing.

Ref.: E-p. 25, H-R91, W-25

65.　[1846]　**Bryant, Edwin**　　　1st: c, 2nd: b
*What I Saw in California: Being the Journal of a Tour, by the
Emigrant Route and South Pass of the Rocky Mountains in the
Years 1846, 1847.* New York: D. Appleton; Philadelphia: S.
Appleton, 1848.
pp. 455

Wagner-Camp-Becker says, "Bryant's is certainly one of the most detailed and reliable of all the overland journals." A second edition was
printed in 1848. A first and second English edition were issued in
London in 1849. Many other printings have followed.

Ref.: C-p. 81, G-457, H-B903, W-26, WC-146

66.　[1843]　**Burnett, Peter Hardeman**　　　1st: bb, rpt.: aa
Recollections and Opinions of an Old Pioneer. New York: Appleton, 1880.
pp. 448 plus 6 pp. ads.
rpt.: An Old California Pioneer, 1946, Oakland, pp. 287,
maps (3), illus.

Burnett traveled in the same company as Applegate, Lenox, and Whitman. He tells of the trip over the plains in 1843 and of his early days
in Oregon and California. *The History of Oregon* by George Wilkes
includes a version, fictionalized, of Burnett's diary (*see* 497). *Also see*
the entry for Nicholas Perkins Hardeman (210), a descendent of Burnett.

Ref.: C-p. 30, G-496, H-B1000, W-29, Z-13

67. [1848] **Burrows, Rufus**   aa
            A Long Road to Stony Creek: Being the Narratives of Rufus
            Burrows and Cyrus Hill, of Their Eventful Lives in the Wilderness
            West of 1848–1858. Ashland: Lewis Osbourne, 1971.
            pp. 70, illus., e-map
A nice printing of these two short, but dramatic, overland narratives.
Burrows, with whom most of this book is concerned, journeyed in the
same company as Pierre Barlow Cornwall and Caleb Greenwood. The
Cyrus Hull account is in the form of letters written later in his life.
They tell of his almost fatal trip to Oregon in 1852.
            Ref.: none

68. [1860] **Burton, Sir Richard F.**   bbb
            The City of Saints and Across the Rocky Mountains to California
            by Richard F. Burton . . . London: Longman, Green, Long-
            man and Roberts, 1861.
            pp. 707, illus., f-map (3 maps on 1 sheet)
            2nd ed.: 1862, same collation
            American ed.: 1862, New York: Harper & Brothers, pp. 574
Even though he only stayed in Utah for approximately a month,
Burton gathered enough information for this book. His travels from
St. Joseph to Salt Lake City took less than a month by stage, and he
later moved on to California.
            Ref.: C-p. 87, G-512, H-B1033, WC-370

69. [1852] **Bushnell, James Addison**   a
            Autobiography of James Addison Bushnell. Eugene, Oreg.: Lane
            County Pioneer Historical Society, 1959.
            pp. 35, port., typescript
Bushnell crossed the plains alone to the California gold diggings. In
1853 he returned to his home in Missouri to find his family had
departed for Oregon. He hurried to Oregon by way of the Isthmus
and met his family near Eugene. Later he started what is now the
Northwest Christian College.
            Ref.: none

70. [1853] **Bushnell, John C.**   a
            Narrative of John C. Bushnell. Eugene, Oreg.: Lane County
            Pioneer Historical Society, 1959.
            pp. 30, port., typescript
John was the brother of James Addison Bushnell, who made the journey overland the previous year. John tells of his experiences in what

he calls the "Lost Wagon Train" which traversed a new route through eastern Oregon to the Willamette Valley in 1853. Many of those involved suffered extreme hardships before reaching the Valley.

Ref.: none

71.   [1852]   **Butler, John Lowe**   a
              Autobiography of John Lowe Butler, 1808–1861 and Other In-
              formation of Interest to His Descendents. N. p.: 1957.
              pp. 58 and appendices

Tells of his experiences from his time in Nauvoo to his later days as Mormon Bishop of Spanish Fork, Utah. Included are his adventures at Winter Quarters and his crossing of the plains to the Salt Lake area.

Ref.: none

72.   [1851]   **Cain, Joseph and Arieh C. Brower**   dd
              Mormon Way-bill, to the Gold Mines, from the Pacific Springs,
              By the Northern & Southern Routes, Viz. Fort Hall, Salt Lake,
              and Los Angelos (sic), including Sublet's, Hudspeth's, and the
              Various Cut-offs . . . G.S.L. City: Deseret, 1851.
              pp. 32   4 or fewer copies known

Sources such as Wagner-Camp-Becker and Howes seem to indicate at least two early editions; one of thirty-two pages, the other with forty. Of the latter, page thirty-nine is blank and page forty, which is not numbered, carries the following note: "This Way-bill is printed on colored paper (brown), being the most durable, and it will not wear out by being creased or carried in the pocket." The forty-page edition contains information on the Oregon Trail from Pacific Springs west-ward. Howes says that this is the first overland guide printed west of Missouri.

Ref.: C-pp. 91–92, G-536, H-C18, WC-196

73.   [1849]   **Caldwell, Dr. T. G. (initials uncertain)**   1st: bbb, anr. ed.:
                                                                    aa
              Notes of a Journey to California by Fort Hall Route, June to Oct.
              1849—Found in Mountains . . . Edited by Georgia Willis Read
              and Ruth Gaines. New York: Columbia University Press, 1944.

This is found on pages 1247 to 1269 in Read and Gaines, *Gold Rush: The Journals, Drawings, and Other Papers of J. Goldsborough Bruff* . . . *April 2, 1849–July 20, 1851.* (see 64). Bruff found the journal in a wagon left with him at his camp in the mountains.

Ref.: H-R91, W-25

74.   [1852]   **Callison, John**   a
              Diary of John Callison. Eugene, Oreg.: Lane County Pioneer
              Historical Society, 1959.
              pp. 10, mounted facs., typescript
Lane County Historical Society states: "The Callison family came from
Scotland to America, living in Virginia, Kentucky, and Hancock County,
Illinois. This diary contains ten pages, with a large print of the first
page of the diary. John Callison died of cholera August 23, 1852, and
his family continued on to the Willamette Valley. Included is a genealogy of the Callison family."
              Ref.: none

75.   [1863]   **Campbell, J. L.**   dd
              *Idaho: Six Months in the New Gold Diggings. The Emigrant's
              Guide Overland. Itinerary of the Routes, Features of the Country,
              Journal of Residence, Etc. Etc.* New York: Tribune Print, 1864.
              Chicago: John R. Walsh, 1864.
              N.Y. ed.: pp. 64, map, 4 plates
              Chi. ed.: pp. 62, map, 4 plates
              anr. ed.: 1865, *Idaho and Montana Gold Regions*
Wagner-Camp-Becker and Howes appear to disagree as to which printing surfaced first, the Chicago or New York publication. Campbell
traveled to Bannack by way of South Pass in 1863. In 1868 an edition
called "Third Annual Edition" appeared with the title, *The Great
Agricultural and Mineral West; A Handbook for the Emigrant.* . . . , (Chicago: Church, Goodman, and Donnelly, pp. 79). Title on the cover:
Campbell's Western Guide.
              Ref.: G-560, H-C297, WC-398

76.   [1853]   **Campbell, Remembrance H.**   cc
              *A Brief History of Our Trip across the Plains with Ox Teams in
              1853.* N. p., n. d. (San Francisco, 1909).
              pp. ?, port., wraps
No copy of this rare pamphlet was located, hence the number of pages
is uncertain. The place and date of printing are also uncertain. Should
a copy surface it may command a higher value than that stated above.
              Ref.: none

77.   [1845]   **Carleton, Lieut. J. Henry**   aaa
              The Prairie Logbooks. Edited by Louis Pelzer. Chicago: Caxton
              Club, 1943.
              pp. 295, maps   350 copies ptd.
Originally published in *The Spirit of the Times,* a New York newspaper,
December 27, 1845 to May 30, 1846. Carleton was under Colonel S.

W. Kearny and traveled with other journalists such as Philip Cooke. Their guide was Fitzpatrick. Carleton's early travels along the Oregon Trail are important for the details he records, and as an outsider's view of the emigrants he encounters. Carleton reports: "These were the first United States troops ever mustered on the Pacific side of the continent . . . ," and most likely bolstered the courage of all emigrants they met. Chapter XIII is concerned with, and titled, "The Oregon Emigrants." Nicely printed and bound.

Ref.: H-C146, WC-120a

78. [1850] **Carr, John**   b
Pioneer Days in California. Eureka, Calif.: Times Publishing Co., 1891.
pp. 452, frontis

The book opens with Judge Carr's account of his overland journey during 1850 in which he speaks of meeting Jim Bridger. Most of the book is involved with California history and politics. The book was reprinted in 1936 in an abridged edition under the title *A Vulcan Among the Argonauts.*

Ref.: C-p. 106, G-590, H-C167, W-35

79. [1843] **Carson, Kit**   aaa
Kit Carson's Own Story of His Life as Dictated to Col. and Mrs. D. C. Peters, about 1856–57, and Never Before Published. Edited by Blanche C. Grant. Taos, 1926.
pp. 138, frontis, wraps, 13 illus.

Kit traveled from Bent's Fort north to the vicinity of Devil's Gate, and from there, in the company of Fremont and Fitzpatrick, on to the Dalles. He tells of their adventures and the Great Salt Lake, and of their later adventures after reaching California, having conquered ". . . barren, desolate and unexplored country."

Ref.: G-603, H-C182

80. [1849] **Carstarphen, James Eula**   aaa
My Trip to California in '49. (Louisiana, Mo., 1914). Limited ed.
pp. 8, port. in text, wraps

A brief account of his overland experience as a member of the "Salt River Tigers" train. Their starting point was New London, Missouri with the gold mines as their destination. His mining pursuits lasted about a year.

Ref.: C-p. 107, G-606

81. [1852] **Carter, E. S.**   d
             The Life and Adventures of E. S. Carter. Including a Trip across
             the Plains in 1852. Indian Wars in the Early Days of Oregon in
             the Years 1854–5–6. St. Joseph, Mo.: Combe Printing Co.,
             1896.
             pp. 145

Carter also includes his life in the California gold fields and his travels
through New Mexico. An exceedingly rare book, it is thought that
most copies were destroyed by fire in the printing office; over the years
only two copies have been offered at a public sale, and are, according
to Howes, the only known copies.

             Ref.: C-p. 835, G-609, H-C186

82. [1856] **(Carter, Kate B., compiler)**   a
             Treasures of Pioneer History. Salt Lake City, 1952.
             pp. 513, map, illus.

This is the first volume in a series concerned with narratives of early
Mormon pioneers. They include the diaries of many who joined the
early Mormon exodus to the West, as well as diaries of some of the
Handcart pioneers of 1856 to 1860, including Camilla W. Judd, Ger-
trude M. Ault, George Cunningham, and many others.

             Ref.: none

83. [1852] **Cartwright, David W. and Mary F. Bailey**   1st: bbb,
                                                            2nd: aaa
             Natural History of Western Wild Animals and Guide for Hunters,
             Trappers, and Sportsmen. . . . Toledo, 1875.
             pp. 280, 19 plates (including frontis)
             2nd ed.: 1875, same collation

Pages 165 to 234 tell of "A tramp to California in 1852." Cartwright,
as a well known hunter of the day, was hired by a Wisconsin group
to guide them to the coast. The title is indicative of the meat of the
book.

             Ref.: C-p. 108, G-616, H-C205

84. [1859] **Casler, Melyer**   ddd
             A Journal Giving the Incidents of a Journey to California in the
             Summer of 1859 by the Overland Route. Toledo: Commercial
             Steam Book and Job, 1863.
             pp. 48
             rpt.: 1969, Fairfield, Wash., pp. 62 (includes facs. of original
                  title page).

Of the two known copies, one is in Yale. A copy was sold in 1957 by the Midland Rare Book Company of Mansfield, Ohio. In this well written contemporary narrative, Casler tells of Salt Lake, the Humboldt, Carson City and Genoa. The rigorous life of a miner proved too much of a strain on the author and he died just a few months after returning to his family in Ohio in early 1862. Casler appears, from his short journal, to be openly honest and warmhearted, and this book may therefore, receive more empathy from the reader than many other narratives of twice the volume.

Ref.: H-C220, WC-385a

85. [1845] **Chambers, Andrew Jackson**   b
          Recollections by Andrew Jackson Chambers. N. p.: 1947.
          pp. 40, stapled

The Chambers family crossed the plains in 1845, wintered at the Dalles, later moved on to Oregon City, and finally settled at Tualatin Plains. Chambers was a participant in the Indian Wars of 1855–56. This very scarce little book was written in 1904, but not printed until 1947, when only a few copies were done.

Ref.: H-C270

86. [1851] **Chambers, Margaret W.**   cc
          Reminisences (sic). N. p.: (1903).
          pp. 48, issued without wraps, wire-stitched

Margaret White Chambers wrote the story of her 1851 overland trip in 1894. She was the wife of Andrew J. Chambers who wrote his own recollections of his crossing in the year 1845. Charles W. Smith in his *Pacific Northwest Americana* locates only two copies of the book, one in the Oregon Historical Society, and the other at the University of Washington Library.

Ref.: G-640, H-C272

87. [1855] **Chandless, William**   bbb
          A Visit to Salt Lake; Being a Journey Across the Plains and a Residence in the Mormon Settlements at Utah. London: Smith, Elder and Co., 1857.
          pp. 346 & 16 (ads.), f-map (map size 15.5 × 28 cm.)

Chandless, a wagon driver from London, traveled from Atchison via the Platte and South Pass to Salt Lake in 1855, and on to Los Angeles in 1856. Although he was only in Salt Lake City for a few months, he found much about the Mormons of interest to write about.

Ref.: C-p. 113, G-646, H-C286, WC-287

88. [1850] **Child, Andrew**   1st: ddd, rpt.: aa
          Overland Route to California, Description of the Route, via Coun-
          cil Bluffs, Iowa; Keeping the North Side of the Platte River . . .
          Thence over South Pass, via the Great Sublette and Bear River
          Cutoffs, and the Truckie River. . . . Milwaukee: Daily Sentinel,
          1852.
          pp. 61
          rpt.: 1946, pp. 60, f-map, plates, 750 copies
Graff states that, "Andrew Child accompanied the Upper Mississippi
Ox Company overland in 1850, with eighty-seven people and thirty-
two wagons. He was one of the few members of the company who
split off at Fort Laramie under the leadership of Vance L. Davidson.
Most of them were from Illinois, Iowa, and Wisconsin." Child's short
directive comments have the result of giving us more of a guidebook
than a record of personal involvement. It is very rare and seldom,
almost never, seen for sale. Therefore, most collectors and interested
historians turn to the reprint of 1946, that includes an introduction
by Lyle H. Wright. Only five copies of the original are known to exist.
          Ref.: G-694, H-C378, W-37, WC-209

89. [1841] **Chiles, Joseph**   a
          A Visit to California in 1841. As recorded by Hubert Howe
          Bancroft. Berkeley: Friends of the Bancroft Library, 1970.
          pp. 23, frontis port., wraps
Chiles traveled overland with the Bidwell-Bartleson party. One of the
great, but generally unheralded, trailblazers of the West.
          Ref.: none

90. [1850] **Christy, Thomas**   a
          Thomas Christy's Road across the Plains. A Guide to the Route
          from Mormon Crossing, Now Omaha, Nebraska, to the City of
          Sacramento, California. . . . Edited by Robert H. Becker.
          Denver: Old West Publishing, 1969.
          pp. 25 and 94, 94 maps
An important addition to any collection concerning the overland
experience. This book combines three elements: Christy's overland
guide and diary printed on one page, with accompanying map illustrating the traced route on each facing page. An interesting introduction by Mr. Becker precedes the overland journey.
          Ref.: none

91. [1853] **Cipriani, Leonetto** aa
California and Overland Diaries of Count Leonetto Cipriani from 1853 through 1871. Containing the Account of His Cattle Drive from Missouri to California in 1853; a Visit to Brigham Young in the Mormon Settlement of Salt Lake City. Edited by Ernest Falbo. Portland: Champoeg Press, 1962.

pp. 153, frontis 750 copies

A nice printing. Cipriani's reminiscence could be called an enigma among overland journals. For instance, well known sites seem non-existent, while mileage estimates are strikingly erroneous. Also in question is the perplexing route taken from Ft. Laramie to South Pass. Cipriani left the wagon train at South Pass to finish the trip alone, terming the venture to that point nothing but a ". . . financial speculation in livestock."

Ref.: P-331

92. [1850] **Clapp, John T.** dd, rpt.: a
A Journal of Travels to and from California with Full Details of the Hardships and Privations; also a Description of the Country, Mines, Cities, Towns, Etc. Kalamazoo, Mich.: Geo. A. Fitch & Co., 1851.

pp. 67, wraps 3 copies known

A rare day-by-day diary, beginning at Council Bluffs, and terminating at Sacramento. Clapp joined the Lake County Company of Illinois led by John G. Ragan. The journal includes a list of seventy-one company members and their addresses. Clapp stayed only until November, returning by boat to Michigan, by way of Panama.

Ref.: C-p. 837, G-726, H-C424, WC-197

93. [1849] **Clark, Bennett C.** aa
Diary of a Journey from Missouri to California in 1849 . . . Edited by Ralph P. Bieber. Columbia, Mo.: State Historical Society, 1928.

pp. 43, port.

Reprinted from the Missouri Historical Review, Vol. 23, No. 1, Oct. 1928. Clark arrived in California in August, after leaving Cooper County in April. See also W. J. Pleasants, *Twice Across the Plains, 1849 . . . 1856.*

Ref.: C-p. 831, G-730

94. [1852] **Clark, John Hawkins**   a
     *Overland to the Gold Fields of California in 1852: The Journal
     of John Hawkins Clark Expanded and Revised from Notes Made
     during the Journey.* Edited by Louise Barry.
     Topeka: Reprinted from the Kansas Historical Quarterly,
              August, 1942. Printed by Kansas State Printing Plant,
              Topeka, 1942.
     pp. 227–296 (numbered thus), port., illus., wraps
A top-notch narrative expanded in his later life from his early journal
notes. One of the strong points of Clark's book is the addition of
many pertinent details concerning the journey. For instance: "Traveled
all night over a desert to make the great meadows of the Humboldt.
Dust and sand as deep and as disagreeable as ever. Were it not for the
wild sage and grease wood those who travel on foot could escape a
great part of the dust, but as the sage and grease wood stand so close
and are so tall that it is impossible through or over them, [we] are
compelled to keep the beaten path, traveling or rather wading through
the deep dust like oxen pushing through deep snow" (p. 285). For the
most part, his entries favor the philosophical and esthetic views of
the experience. One of the photos included is a rare 1866 scene of
Ft. Bridger.
     Ref.: none

95. [1849] **Clark, Sterling B. F.**   a
     How Many Miles From St. Jo. San Francisco, 1929.
     pp. 56, frontis, 4 plates
A handsome little book containing the somewhat engaging jottings
of an overland journal, plus the brief memoirs of this early San Francisco merchant. Printed in a limited edition.
     Ref.: G-742, W-40

96. [1847] **Clayton, William**   aaa
     *William Clayton's Journal: A Daily Record of the Journey of the
     Original Company of "Mormon" Pioneers from Nauvoo to Salt
     Lake.* Salt Lake City, 1921.
     pp. 376, port.
Clayton was "historian" of the Mormon overland party of 1847, and
kept a daily journal in which were recorded the events of the expedition, together with observations on the country and Indian tribes
that might prove valuable to following members. An index was done
in Salt Lake City in 1942, consisting of 28 pages.
     Ref.: H-C474

97. [1847] **Clayton, William** ddd
The Latter-Day Saints' Emigrants' Guide; Being a Table of Distances. St. Louis: Chambers and Knapp, 1848.
pp. 24
rpt.: (facs.) 1921, Salt Lake City, pp. 24
This was the best guidebook from Council Bluffs to the Great Salt Lake area. It was used extensively by the Mormons (among others) during their migration. John D. Lee, in 1848, used the guide; apparently so did Lorenzo Snow as several of his place names are identical with Clayton's.
Ref.: G751, H-C475, WC-147

98. [1864] **Clinkinbeard, Philura V.** a
Across the Plains in '64, by Prairie Schooner to Oregon. From the Stories of Her Mother, Philura V. Clinkenbeard, compiled and arranged by Anna Dell Clinkinbeard. New York: Exposition Press (1953).
pp. 97
Possibly printed in a small number. Possibly sales and distribution were lacking. Whatever the reason, this somewhat modern printing is extremely difficult to locate.
Ref.: none

99. [1844] **Clyman, James** 1st: c, rpt.: aaa
James Clyman, American Frontiersman. Edited by Charles L. Camp. San Francisco: California Historical Society, 1928.
pp. 251, 3 maps, port., illus.
rpt.: with much added, 1960, Portland. pp. 400, 17 maps and plates, 1000 copies printed.
This is the only overland journal to Oregon for this year. The emigration consisted of about 1500 plus a small party led by Elisha Stephens. This was the Stephens-Murphy group that took the Ft. Hall cutoff to California. An important and interesting journal written by one of the most fascinating of frontiersmen.
Ref.: C-p. 132, G-769, H-C81, Z-19

100. [1850] **Coke, Henry J.** bbb
A Ride over the Rocky Mountains to Oregon and California. With a Glance at some of the Tropical Islands, including the West Indies and the Sandwich Islands. London: Richard Bentley, 1853.
pp. 388, frontis port.
One of the most stimulating of all overland narratives, and one of the West's best adventure stories. Apparently Coke, and a small group of young adventurers, traveled from St. Louis to the Dalles for the sheer

excitement. The result was a perilous journey during which two died. Based on their inexperience (their food supply included ginger beer and chocolate) and lack of cohesiveness (they broke into two- and three-man parties), it remains a wonder that Coke survived the experience. He speaks of meeting Kit Carson on the Sweetwater, and does his best to pass on to the reader the novelty and excitement of his adventures along the road to Oregon.

Ref.: C-p. 134, G-796, H-C548, W-44, WC-211

101.   [1852]   **Cole, Gilbert L.**   aa
In the Early Days along the Overland Trail in Nebraska Territory in 1852 . . . Kansas City: Franklin Hudson Publishers, 1905. pp. 125, port.

Cole, a member of the small train of Capt. Wadsworth, journeyed overland from Michigan to California. There is an abundance of human interest in this well written adventure. Compiled by Mrs. A. Hardy.

Ref.: G-801, H-C2102 (1954 ed.)

102.   [1864]   **Collins, John S.**   1st: bb, 2nd ed.: bbb
Across the Plains in '64: Incidents of the Early Days West of the Missouri River, and of the Pioneer Period. Omaha, 1904. pp. 151

2nd ed: 1911, Omaha, pp. 151 and 152, port., 2 vols. in 1

The second edition, containing two volumes, is considered the more desirable. The 1904 edition is reported to have been printed for friends only, with no copies being offered for sale. The second printing was done after Mr. Collins's death fulfilling the wishes of the will. It was bound up with the undistributed copies of the first edition and distributed according to his wishes. A pertinent book for information on overland travels. Collins, after crossing South Pass, took Lander's cutoff to Virginia City. He was post trader at Ft. Laramie for ten years. A very difficult book to find.

Ref.: G-809 and 810, H-C594

103.   [1848]   **Cook, Phineas W.**   aa
The Life and History of Phineas W. Cook. N. p., N. d. pp. 120

When his ox died Cook hitched up with the infamous Porter Rockwell for the finish of his journey to Salt Lake City. Cook says he wrote this "for the good of my posterity."

Ref.: none

104. [1852] **Cooke, Lucy R.** aaa
> *Crossing the Plains in 1852. Narrative of a Trip from Iowa to "The Land of Gold" as Told in Letters Written during the Journey . . .* Modesto, Calif., 1923.
> pp. 94, 2 plates, wraps

Title on wrapper: "Covered Wagon Days. Crossing the plains in 1852 by Lucy Rutledge Cooke." Lucy was a member of the Dubuque Emigration Co. Graff says "composed almost entirely of letters written by Mrs. Cooke to her sister in 1852 and 1853, the narrative is a vivid account of an overland trip, events along the way, her nine-month stay in Salt Lake City, and an amusing proposal made by a Mormon elder." A scarce book.
> Ref.: C-p. 839, G-868, H-C737, P-377

105. [1845] **Cooke, Lieut. Col. Philip** bbb
> *Scenes and Adventures in the Army.* Philadelphia: Lindsay & Blakiston, 1857.
> pp. 432
> rpt.: 1859, same, with Cooke now "Colonel."

Cooke was with Kearny's command to escort emigrants going to Oregon. See also the entry by Carleton, another member of the same escort.
> Ref.: G-871, H-C740, WC-288

106. [1853] **Cornaby, Hannah L.** aaa
> *Autobiography and Poems.* Salt Lake City, 1881.
> pp. 158

This reminiscence was written during the author's last years. It records her trip by oxcart from Keokuk, Iowa to Salt Lake City, and her life in the area.
> Ref.: none

107. [1848] **(Cornwall, Bruce)** b
> *Life Sketch of Pierre Barlow Cornwall.* San Francisco: pvt. ptd., 1906.
> pp. 87, 6 ports., including frontis

Cornwall, in the company of his brother and Tom Fallon, the well known trapper and scout, left St. Joseph in April of 1848 overland for California. After enduring many severe hardships he arrived in Sacramento, where he later made his fortune. Cornwall served as president of the Society of California Pioneers. This biography is by his son, Bruce, and the overland trip covers only a few pages. An attractive book.
> Ref.: C-p. 143, G-880, H-C780

108.   [1860]   **Crane, Ellery P.**   aaa
       An Overland Trip to California in 1860. Worchester Society of
       Antiquity, 1901.
       pp. 21, wraps
This is the journey of a small group that left Omaha on the Fifth of
June. Crane describes the difficulties and dangers met with while
traveling the Platte to Salt Lake City, and from there over the deserts
of Nevada. Quite scarce.
       Ref.: none

109.   [1851]   **Crawford, Charles H.**   b
       *Scenes of Earlier Days in Crossing the Plains to Oregon, and
       Experiences of Western life.* Petaluma, Calif.: J. T. Studdert,
       1898.
       pp. 186, frontis port., illus.
Crawford was a member of the Hadley party. This somewhat crudely
printed narrative tells of starting in April and reaching their destination in August after a good dose of Indian trouble.
       Ref.: C-p. 149, G-911, H-C870

110.   [1842]   **Crawford, Medorem**   aa
       *An Account of His Trip across the Plains with the Oregon Pioneers
       of 1842.* Eugene, Oreg.: Star Job Office, 1897.
       pp. 26
This is the only diary kept of the first large emigrant train to Oregon.
Crawford was a member of Elijah White's party, and traveled with
Meek and Hastings. This is the first separate printing of the narrative
that was issued in 1863 as a government document (*Journal of the
Expedition Organized for the Protection of Emigrants to Oregon . . .* U.S.
37th Congress, 3rd Session, Ex. Doc. 17). Crawford also reportedly
traveled overland again in 1863. The year, 1842, is erroneously printed
in Howes as 1862.
       Ref.: G-914, H-C874

111.   [1856]   **Cropper, Thomas W.**   a
       *Family History of Thomas W. Cropper and Hannah Lucretia
       Rogers, Also Short Sketches . . .* Edited by Robert L. Ashley.
       N. p., (1957).
       pp. 37
Cropper's mother, following the death of his father in 1851, became
converted to Mormonism and started for Utah in 1853. Upon hearing

of the practice of polygamy she turned back and married a gentile.
Cropper finally made it to Utah in 1856 traveling between two of the
handcart companies. Upon his arrival he found employment as a stone
hauler for the temple at Salt Lake City.

Ref.: none

112. [1849] **Cross, Osborne**   1st: cc, Sen. ed.: b, Wash. ed.: aaa,
                                                            1940 ed.: aa
                A Report in the Form of a Journal, the March of the Regiment of
                Mounted Riflemen to Oregon from May 10 to October 5, 1849.
                Philadelphia: C. Sherman, 1850.
                pp. 228, f-map, illus. (map size, 52 × 48 cm.), 36 plates
                anr. ed.: in *Report of the Quartermaster General for 1850*, (Sen.
                    Exec. Doc. 1) in which it is pages 126–244, 34 to
                    37 plates (editions vary)
                anr. ed.: 1850, Wash., no map
                rpt.: as *March of the Mounted Riflemen*, 1940, Raymond Set-
                    tle, Arthur H. Clark Co.

The whole report revolves around the trip over the trail and Cross
gives the reader one of the best descriptions of it. He speaks of the
emigrants and their problems, as well as relating on a regular basis his
own troubles with his men, the trail, and the many undernourished
animals in his company. For another version, see George Gibbs journal
in the 1940 printing by the Arthur H. Clark Co.

Ref.: G-4415, H-C923, WC-181

113. [1857] **Cumming, Elizabeth**   a
                The Genteel Gentile. Letters of Elizabeth Cumming, 1857–1858.
                Edited by Ray R. Canning and Beverly Beeton. Salt Lake
                City: Tanner Trust Fund, University of Utah, (1977).
                pp. 111, frontis port., illus., e-maps   1250 copies

She accompanied the Utah Expedition as wife of Alfred Cumming,
who was appointed by President Buchanan as the first non-Mormon
governor of Utah. Even though she encountered many difficult mo-
ments along the trail, including being forced to spend the winter near
Ft. Bridger, Elizabeth writes of this time as being the "happiest and
pleasantest months" of her life. Nicely printed.

Ref.: none

114. [1845] **Cummins, Mrs. Sarah J.**   aaa, other eds.: aa
     Autobiography and Reminiscences.
     *N. p., (1914), pp. 61, ports.
     **La Grande, Oreg.: (1914), pp. 63, frontis port.
     Freewater, Oreg.: (Mrs. J. J. Allen), 1914, pp. 61, illus.
     Cleveland: Arthur H. Clark Co., 1914, pp. 63
     Touchet, Wash.: 1914.
     Walla Walla: Walla Walla Bulletin (1914), pp. 61
     *Charles W. Smith's *Pacific Northwest Americana* indicates this to be
the first printing. **Howe lists this as the first printing (the only
printing he lists). This is a somewhat impetuous but enthralling account of the near-demise of Sarah when she was a teenage bride
crossing the plains. She speaks of Fremont traveling with them for a
short time, being saved from hostile Indians in Sioux country, and
adds a bit about the Yellowstone area. Apparently she was in the same
train as William Goulder, Samuel Hancock, and Solomon Tethrow.
She wrote this as she was nearing ninety.
     Ref.: G-949, H-C952

115. [1849] **Dameron, James Palatine**   bb
     Autobiography and Writings of J. P. Dameron. (San Francisco,
     1877).
     pp. 31, double columns, wraps
     A rare account of an overland trip in 1849. Graff did not have a copy
and Howes, if he knew of this item, did not include it in US-iana.
Seldom seen for sale.
     Ref.: C-p. 154

116. [1850] **Davis, Henry T.**   aa
     *Solitary Places Made Glad . . . Experiences for Thirty-two Years
     in Nebraska.* Cincinnati: Printed for the Author, 1890.
     pp. 422, port.
     Although Davis crossed the plains, this deals mostly with his other
experiences.
     Ref.: C-p. 841, G-1018, H-D114

117. [1853] **Davis, John E.**   1st.: bbb, rpts.: aaa
     *Mormonism Unveiled; a Peep into the Principles . . . by . . . a
     Deluded Brother of the Sect. . . .* Bristol: C. T. Jefferies, 1855.
     pp. 48
     rpt.: 1856, Bristol, pp. 24; 1858, Cardiff (3rd ed.)

Davis traveled overland from "Cainsville" to Salt Lake City in 1853 with a group of Mormons. He wrote this exposé upon deciding to leave Mormonism after "recovering from his infatuation."

Ref.: H-D124, WC-273b

118. [1841]   **Dawson, Nicholas "Cheyenne"**   1st: d, rpt.: aaa
California in '41. Texas in '51. (Austin, 1901).
pp. 119, port.   50 copies ptd.
rpt.: *Narrative of . . . "Cheyenne Dawson"* San Francisco:
        Grabhorn Press, 1933, pp. 100, colored drawings.

Dawson was a member of the Bidwell-Bartleson party. He acquired the nickname "Cheyenne" after an embarrassing encounter with the Indians during the journey overland. An important reminiscence, Dawson's was the last one written by a member of the 1841 party. Only two or three copies are known of the original fifty printed for family and friends (Texas State Library and California State Library have copies).

Ref.: C-p. 161, G-1027, H-D159

119. [1852]   **Dean, Thaddeus**   a
A Journey to California, the Letters of Thaddeus Dean. Edited by Katherine Dean Wheeler. Tampa: American Studies Press, 1979.
pp. 26, frontis, wraps

An interesting and personal view of a man's experiences, drawn from letters written by the editor's father, Thaddeus Dean.

Ref.: none

120. [1849]   **Decker, Peter**   aa
Diaries of Peter Decker. Overland to California in 1849 and Life in the Mines, 1850–1851. Edited by Helen Giffen. George-town, Calif.: Talisman Press, 1966.
pp. 338, f-map, frontis, illus. (map size, 15 × 42 cms.)

Decker speaks in glowing terms of the many scenic variations along the route. He also gives a fairly detailed version of the problems encountered and endured, particularly in crossing the Nevada deserts. His party was called the "Columbus California Industrial Association" and traveled, after reaching South Pass, by way of Sublette's cutoff, Ft. Hall, and the Carson River. Decker's narrative does not read as smoothly as some other narratives, but more than makes up for this slight defect with an interesting and detailed report of the journey of 1849.

Ref.: none

121. [1849] **Delano, Alonzo**   1st: cc, best rpt.: aa
      *Life on the Plains and Among the Diggings; Being Scenes and
      Adventures of an Overland Journey to California: with Particular
      Incidents of the Route, Mistakes and Sufferings of the Emi-
      grants* . . . Auburn and Buffalo, Orton & Mulligan, 1854.
      pp. 384, frontis, 3 engraved plates
      best rpt.: 1936, New York, Wilson-Erickson Pub., pp. 191
The first edition, first issue, has page 219 misnumbered "119" and
carries "Sterotyped by Derby and Miller, Auburn" on the copyright
page. This may be the most interesting of all early California overland
books. Delano arrived via the Lassen-Applegate trail across the Black
Rock desert and over the Sierra to Goose Lake. He later wrote under
the name of "Old Block."
      Ref.: G-1042, H-D230, W-57, WC-238

122. [1849] **De Milt, Alonzo**   aaa
      *The Life, Travels, and Adventures of an American Wanderer: A
      Truthful Narrative of Events in the Life of Alonzo De Milt Con-
      taining His Early Adventures* . . . Edited by Franklyn Fitch.
      New York: John W. Lovell, (1883).
      pp. 228 and 48 (ads.), port., plates
Consists of De Milt's journal of an expedition across the plains in
1849. He also includes stories of life among the goldseekers, and
comments on the Mormons and the Donner party. Imaginative.
      Ref.: C-p. 213, G-1338, H-F156

123. [1851] **Denny, Arthur A.**   1st: bb, rpt.: aaa
      Pioneer Days on Puget Sound. Seattle: C. B. Bagley, Printer,
      1888.
      pp. 83, errata slip
      rpt.: 1903, same imprint, pp. 103, 36 plates, 850 copies
Denny traveled from Illinois to the Oregon Territory in 1851, leaving
in April and arriving in August. He gives a history of the area, including information on pioneer and Indian problems. Howes says that
many copies of the first edition were burned. Unfortunately, he adds
no additional information as to how many of the books that might
have been.
      Ref.: G-1053, H-D253a

124. [1841] **De Smet, Pierre-Jean**   ccc
      *Letters and Sketches; with a Narrative of a Year's Residence among
      Indian Tribes of the Rocky Mountains.* Philadelphia: M. Fithian,
      1843.
      pp. 252, frontis & 11 plates

Traveled with the Bidwell-Bartleson party as far as Ft. Hall. From there he went north to the Flathead Indian territory on the upper Columbia. Published again; 1843, Phil. with 244 pages. There was also a french ed., *Voyages aux Montagnes Rocheuses*, pp. 304, map, port., 18 plates, 1844. There were many more eds.

Ref.: G-3823, H-D283, WC-102

125. [1846]   **(Dickenson, Luella)**   ccc
             *Reminiscences of a Trip across the Plains in 1846 and Early Days
             in California.* San Francisco: Whitaker & Ray Co., 1904.
             pp. 118, frontis port., ports., plates
             rpt.: 1977, Fairfield, pp. 48

The Dickenson party was the last wagon train to get over the Sierra Mountains in 1846, the year the Donners were stopped by the snow. The trip was made by Luella's husband, who was the son of G. D. Dickenson, captain of the party. Mrs. Dickenson wrote this book from the information provided by her husband. A copy of the book sold at the Dr. Henry W. Plath auction by the Parke-Bernet Galleries in 1959 for $200.00.

Ref.: C-p. 168, G1078, H-D318

126. [1864]   **(Dickson, Arthur Jerome, Ed.)**   aa
             *Covered Wagon Days. A Journey across the Plains in the Sixties,
             and Pioneer Days in the Northwest; From the Private Journals of
             Albert Jerome Dickson.* Cleveland: Arthur H. Clark Co., 1929.
             pp. 275, f-map, illus.

This is one of the best overland narratives. The chapter titled "A Diversion" tells, perhaps more poignantly than any other journal, how much any small dose of entertainment meant to those traveling the plains month after month; and just how it felt to be there by the night time fire enjoying the "diversion." Dickson's party turned north at Ft. Hall for the diggings at Virginia City, Montana. Included also are some interesting comments about the area's outlaws: Plummer, Slade, etc. Dickson was a young boy when he wrote this.

Ref.: G-1082

127. [1853]   **Dinwiddie, David or John**   a
             Overland from Indiana to Oregon, the Dinwiddie Journal. Edited
             by Margaret Booth. Missoula: Montana State University, 1928.
             pp. 14

This is believed to have been written by David or John Dinwiddie. It is the second in a series of historical reprints, *Sources of Northwest History.* Reprinted from the historical section of "The Frontier," a magazine of the Northwest; Vol. VIII, No. 2, March, 1928. Also reprinted in *Frontier Omnibus*, 1962, Montana State University Press, John W. Hakola, ed., pages 181–195. It is a contemporary diary of some interest.

Ref.: none

128. [1849] **Disturnell, John**   d
             The Emigrants Guide to New Mexico, California, and Oregon.
             New York: J. Disturnell, 1849.
             pp. 46, f-map (of North America) (map size, 14.5 × 9.5 cms.)

Another edition featured a map of California, New Mexico, and "Adjacent Countries" and was also dated 1849. In 1850 the third printing carried the date along with a map of North America. All three editions are rare.

Ref.: H-D351, WC-167a

129. [1853] **Drake, F. M.**   ddd
             *The Emigrant's Overland Guide to California by F. M. Drake
             of Iowa.* Ft. Madison: Evangelist Book and Job Office, 1853.
             pp. 16

According to Wagner-Camp-Becker, there is only one known copy of this guidebook. It is at Yale and lacks a front wrapper.

Ref.: WC-222b

130. [1853] **Draper, Elias J.**   bbb
             *An Autobiography of Elias J. Draper a Pioneer of California,
             Containing Some Thrilling Incidents Relating to Crossing the Plains
             by Ox Team, and Some Very Interesting Particulars of Life in
             California in the Early Days* . . . Fresno: Evening Democrat
             Print, 1904.
             pp. 76, port.

Draper tells of making the long journey over the plains in 1853 and again in 1858. A very scarce book.

Ref.: C-p. 183, G-1149, H-D484

131. [1864] **(Draper, Mabel Hobson)**   a
             Though Long the Trail. New York, 1946.
             pp. 313, frontis port.

The author tells the story her mother, Mary Quinn Hobson, told her concerning her trip over the Oregon Trail as a small girl. The author attempts to retell the story as her mother would have, and uses down homesy dialogue. She states her mother had a "big bump of curiosity" and everything she experienced interested her.

Ref.: none

132. [1854] **Drumheller, "Uncle Dan"** b
Tells Thrills of Western Trails in 1854. Spokane: pvt. ptg., 1925.
pp. 142, ports.

"Uncle Dan" was a pioneer stockman and banker, and gives a very
brief report of his journey overland from the southwestern Missouri
town of Springfield to the Sacramento Valley. He states it took him
only 152 days to complete the trip.
Ref.: G-1158, H-D511

133. [1849] **Dundass, Samuel R.** dd
*Journal of Samuel Rutherford Dundass . . . Including His Entire
Route to California, as a Member of the Steubenville Company
Bound for San Francisco, in the Year 1849.* Steubenville, Ohio:
Conn's Job Office, 1857.
pp. 60, wraps

This journal was published after Dundass died of typhoid in Buffalo,
N.Y., upon returning from California in 1850. The Steubenville Com-
pany was composed of sixty natives of Ohio, and traveled by way of
South Pass to Salt Lake, then across the terrible Hastings cutoff to
the Humboldt. Only about a dozen copies are known to exist.
Ref.: C-p. 187, G-1178, H-D566, WC-290

134. [1864] **Dunham, E. Allene Taylor** bbb
Across the Plains in a Covered Wagon. N. p., n. d.
pp. 20, wraps

Mrs. Dunham started in Iowa and journeyed to California in 1864.
This is a scarce overland narrative probably printed, according to
Graff, during the 1920's.
Ref.: G-1179

135. [1852] **Duniway, Mrs. Abigail J.** dd
*Captain Gray's Company; or Crossing the Plains and Living in
Oregon.* Portland: S. J. McCormick, 1859.
pp. 342

According to Howes, the author seems to have written a romantic
novel concerned with an 1850 overland trip, basing it on her own
experiences while crossing the plains in 1852. This is the first literary
work written and printed in Oregon and is a very difficult book to
find in a first edition. Mrs. Duniway also wrote: *From the West to the
West. Across the Plains to Oregon* (1905, Chicago, pp. 311, frontis).
This is another, and more romanticized, telling of her trip, written
many years after the above named book.
Ref.: G-1180, H-D568, WC-323

136. [1864] **Dunlop, Kate** a

The Montana Gold Rush Diary of Kate Dunlop. Edited by S. Lyman Tyler. Denver and Salt Lake City: Old West Publishing, 1969.

pp. (7) A-8 to A-15, (41) B-2 to B-43, (13) C-2 to C-15, 22 maps, illus.

This beautifully printed book from Fred Rosenstock is unusual in at least two aspects. It contains colored maps illustrating the route, and lines from the accompanying diary to the site of the camp, as depicted on a map, for each day. The diary section of the book reads from the back of the book toward the front (east to west), in order to give the reader the same sense of direction in reading the diary as experienced by the author as she recorded it. The journey is by way of the Platte River, South Pass, and Lander's Cutoff to Bannack.

Ref.: none

137. [1852] **Dunn, Mary M.** aaa

Undaunted Pioneers Ever Moving Onward—Westward and Homeward (As Told to Mary E. Stevens). (Eugene: 1929).

pp. 54, illus., wraps

Mary's reminiscences include her arrival in Athens, Mo., by boat from Tennessee, and her overland experiences to Oregon.

Ref.: none

138. [1863] **Edgerton, Mary** a

A Governor's Wife on the Mining Frontier. The Letters of Mary Edgerton from Montana 1863–1865. Edited by James L. Thane Jr. Salt Lake City: Tanner Trust Fund, 1976.

pp. 148, frontis port., photos, e-maps   1250 copies

Mary's husband Sidney was appointed Chief Justice of the new Idaho Territory in 1863. The couple made a "long, uncomfortable, and difficult" overland trip through South Pass from Omaha, settling in Bannack. Her diary is in the form of letters with helpful additions inserted strategically by the editor, James L. Thane Jr. Nicely printed.

Ref.: none

139. [1842] **Edwards, Philip Leget** rpt.: aaa

Sketch of the Oregon Territory or, Emigrants' Guide. Liberty, Mo.: Printed at the "Herald" Office, 1842.

pp. 20

rpt.: (1953, Kansas?) 500 copies

also: (1953, Columbus, Ohio)

This was the first of many guidebooks designed to give advice to those journeying west. Edwards made the trip in 1834 with Wyeth and spent four years in the Oregon Territory. The only known copy is at Yale

University Library. Before reaching the library shelf it had been owned, at different times, by bookmen, Herschel V. Jones, Edward Eberstadt, and Wiliam Coe.

Ref.: H-E67, WC-89

140. [1847] **Egan, Howard R.**   aa
Pioneering in the West 1846–78. Richmond, Utah: Howard R. Egan Estate, 1917.
pp. 303, illus.

The Egan family traveled from Nauvoo with the Mormons. Howard later became a pony express and overland mail agent, and pioneered new trails to the Pacific. Page 303 is an illustration.

Ref.: E-p. 53, G-1221, H-E76

141. [1849] **(Ellenbecker, John G.)**   aaa
The Jayhawkers of Death Valley. Marysville, Kans., 1938.
pp. 130, double columns, photos, pictorial covers

A sought after book that covers material not found in the Manly or Stephens narratives. It follows the trail overland from Galesburg, through Salt Lake City to California. This book also contains the fragmentary diary of Asa Haynes, not found elsewhere.

Ref.: E-p. 53, H-E91

142. [1853] **Ellmaker, Enos**   a
Autobiography of Enos Ellmaker (Rewritten by Amos F. Ellmaker). Eugene, Oreg.: Lane County Historical Society, 1962.
pp. 16, and (unnumbered) 39, ports., wraps, ptd. on rectos only

Ellmaker recorded a brief, piecemeal narrative of his 1853 journey from Iowa to Oregon. The unnumbered section includes letters from Reuben Ellmaker, Enos's brother, still living in Iowa. Much background history is given regarding the Ellmaker (Oelmacher) family.

Ref.: none

143. [1850] **Enos, A. A.**   bbb
Across the Plains in 1850. Stanton, Nebr.: pvt. ptd., (1905).
(date uncertain)
pp. 56, wraps

This account was first published in the newspaper *The Stanton Picket.* Enos traveled from Indiana to the area of Hangtown. His description of the journey includes the Pawnee Indians skinning a man alive in Nebraska, and his impressions of the notable spots along the trail. This overland narrative is very hard to find as only a few copies are known to exist. Measurements are 24 by 16.3 cm.

Ref.: G-1252, H-E160

144.   [1861]   **(Escher, Louise, Ed.)**   aa
                 Across the Plains in 1861. Hollywood, 1922. (place uncertain)
                 pp. 15, port., wraps
       This is the account of a trip by Harrison Paup from Iowa to Nevada.
       A biographical history of Paup runs from page five to page seven.
                 Ref.: none

145.   [1859]   **Evans, Robley D.**   aa
                 A Sailor's Log. Recollections of Forty Years of Naval Life. New
                 York, 1901.
                 pp. 462, illus.
       Evans tells in two chapters, of his journey as a young man overland
       to Utah. He relates experiences along the way, including those in-
       volving Washakie and Brigham Young.
                 Ref.: none

146.   [1849]   **Fairchild, Lucius**   a
                 California Letters of Lucius Fairchild. Edited by Joseph Schafer.
                 Madison: State Historical Society, 1931.
                 pp. 212, illus., port.
       These are informative letters covering both Fairchild's 1849 sojourn
       overland and his subsequent life in the gold areas. They give a moving
       picture of the man, his thoughts, and the events of that era.
                 Ref.: W-70

147.   [1858]   **Farmer, J. E.**   a
                 My Life with the Army in the West/Memoirs of J. E. Farmer.
                 Edited by Dale F. Giese. Santa Fe: Stagecoach Press, 1967.
                 pp. 83, frontis   750 copies
       The introduction states that Farmer wrote this at the age of eighty-
       one. He traveled as a teenage member of the Army over the plains
       to Camp Floyd, Utah, as part of the American force sent to quell the
       Mormon disturbances. A pleasing memoir, and nicely printed.
                 Ref.: none

148.   [1850]   **Ferguson, Charles D.**   b
                 *The Experiences of a Forty-niner during Thirty-four Years' Resi-
                 dence in California and Australia . . .* Edited by Frederick T.
                 Wallace. Cleveland: Williams Publishing Co., 1888.
                 pp. 507, 30 woodcuts
       Ferguson worked in such California mining towns as Nevada City, and
       (on the Feather River) Gold Run. He describes his overland sojourn

via South Pass and Salt Lake City, which he actually undertook in 1850. Cowan also records *The Experiences of a Forty-niner during a Third of a Century in the Gold Fields,* by Charles D. Ferguson. Chico, Calif.: H. A. Carson, 1924, 154 pages.

Ref.: C-p. 206, G-1305, W-74

149. [1852] **Ferris, Benjamin G.** 1st: aaa, rpt.: aa
Utah and the Mormons . . . from Personal Observation during a Six Month's Residence at Great Salt Lake City . . . New York: Harper & Brothers, Publishers, 82 Beekman St., 1854.
pp. 347, frontis, 24 plates
rpt.: 1856, New York, pp. 377

The plates include many of the well known overland scenes such as Chimney Rock and Devil's Gate, plus a number of scenes of Mormon life. His wife Cornelia wrote about her trip to Salt Lake City and her journey to California in 1853. (*See* 150.)

Ref.: H-F98, WC-238b

150. [1852] **Ferris, Mrs. Benjamin G.** aaa
The Mormons at Home; With Some Incidents of Travel from Missouri to California, 1852–3, in a series of Letters. New York: Dix & Edwards, 321 Broadway. London: Sampson Low, Son & Co., 1856
pp. 299

Cornelia went from Independence to California via Salt Lake City, the Humboldt, and the Carson route. She was the wife of the author of *Utah and the Mormons.*

Ref.: C-p. 207, G-1308, H-F99, WC-274

151. [1843] **Field, Matthew C.** a
Prairie and Mountain Sketches. Edited by Kate L. Gregg and John F. McDermott. Norman: University of Oklahoma Press, 1957.
pp. 239, map, frontis (in color), illus., some of which are paintings by A. J. Miller.

The author was a correspondent who traveled with William Drummond on his adventures into Wyoming and back. Of special interest are early names and inscriptions copied from Independence Rock. These reports were originally published in the newspaper. This is the first printing in book form.

Ref.: WC-104

152. [1851] **(Fielding, Mrs. Harriet Chapin)** a
The Ancestors and Descendents of Isaac Alden and Irene Smith,
His Wife (1599–1903). East Orange, N.J., 1903.
pp. 144, frontis, ports., facs.
In this family history compiled by Mrs. Fielding, pages 45 to 49 contain
the brief account of an overland journey in 1851 by Wyllis Alden.
Ref.: G-1317

153. [1850] **Fish, Joseph** a
The Life and Times of Joseph Fish, Mormon Pioneer. Edited by
John H. Krenkel. (Danville: Interstate Printers, 1970).
pp. 518, frontis port., end maps
One of the most complete recordings of early Mormon events by a
well traveled participant. After his crossing of the plains he settled in
Centerville, Utah. Soon after he moved to Parowan, and later on to
Snowflake, Arizona.
Ref.: none

154. [1847] **Fisher, Rachel** a
Covered Wagon Women. Edited by Kenneth L. Holmes. Glendale: Arthur H. Clark Co., 1983.
pp. 272, frontis, f-map, errata slip
The Fisher letters are found in Volume I of this ten-part series devoted
to previously unpublished, or quite rare, diaries and letters. The editor
describes the letters as "poignant" and indeed they are. Rachel tells
of losing her husband along the Platte, and of the death of her young
daughter in Idaho.
Ref.: none

155. [1860] **Fjeld, Carl Johan** a
Brief History of the Fjeld-Fields Family, Compiled and Written
by Andrew Field. (Springville, Utah: Art City, 1946).
pp. 273
Fjeld emigrated to America, journeyed to St. Joseph by train, and
then as the leader of the third division handcart company, crossed
the plains to Utah in 1860.
Ref.: none

156. [1850] **Flake, Lucy Hannah W.** a
To the Last Frontier: Autobiography of Lucy Hannah White Flake.
(Mesa, n. d.) (place uncertain)
pp. 233, typed on recto only

Davis Bitton, in his *Mormon Diaries & Autobiographies*, calls this "an impressive autobiography." After traveling to Utah and marrying William Flake, Lucy and her husband were called upon to help colonize Arizona. Their settlement, named by Erastus Snow, is Snowflake.

Ref.: none

157. [1853] **(Fletcher, Daniel C.)** b
Reminiscences of California and the Civil War. Ayer, Mass.: Huntley S. Turner, 1894.

pp. 196, frontis

Fletcher traveled by boat to California in 1852 and spent a number of years among the mining camps, including Gold Hill, Grass Valley, and Rough and Ready. He tells of his brothers' cattle drive over the plains, and gives details of their trip in 1853.

Ref.: C-p. 214, G-1350, H-F188

158. [1844] **(Foote, H. S.)** b
Pen Pictures from the Garden of the World. Chicago: Lewis Publishing, 1888.

pp. 637, frontis port., map, ports., illus.

Contains local history and biographies including notices on several members of the Stevens-Murphy party. Most important of these is an account of the journey under the subtitle, "Story of the Murphy Party." This is the narrative of Moses Schallenberger, originally written for Hubert Howe Bancroft about 1885.

Ref.: none

159. [1849] **Foster, Charles** d
The Gold Placers of California, with . . . the Routes and Distances There . . . to Which is Added a Method of Assaying Gold . . . Akron: H. Canfield, 1849.

pp. 106, f-map in six sections (map size, 53.2 × 13.9 cms.)

"The preface, dated February 15, 1849, indicates that this gold rush guide was one of the first to reach the public. Camp, however, doubted that it antedated those by Ware and Newhall."—Wagner-Camp-Becker. Pages 53–54, 57–58, 61–62, 95–96, and 99–100 are out of order.

Ref.: H-F282, WC-167d

160. [1848] **Foster, George G.**   bbb
     The Gold Regions of California: Being a Succinct Description of
     the Geography, Topography, and General Features of Califor-
     nia. . . New York: DeWitt and Davenport, 1848.
     pp. 80 and 12 (ads.), frontis map, wraps
     2nd ed.: 1848, stated "Second Edition"
     3rd ed.: 1848, stated "Third Edition"
Foster's map for this early guidebook is one of the first to mention the
"Gold Region." It appears he compiled this book from many sources
including Farhham, Emory, and the "Californian." Another edition,
titled *The Gold Mines of California*, also 1848, is according to Howes
the first printing.
     Ref.: C-p. 219, G-1387, H-F287

161. [1849] **(Foster, Mrs. Roxanna C., Ed.)** 1st: bb, rev. ed.: bbb
     The Foster Family, California Pioneers. San Jose, (1889).
     pp. 46, frontis
     rev. ed.: 1925, Santa Barbara, with added journal (via Pan-
        ama), pp. 285
Contains three journals of the Foster Family, 1849, 1852, and 1853.
The 1849 journal is by Isaac Foster who left Plainfield, Illinois on the
26th of March and returned from California, sometime later, by way
of Panama.
     Ref.: C-p. 847, G-1390, H-F292

162. [1854] **Francl, Joseph**   aa
     The Overland Journey of Joseph Francl, the First Bohemian to
     Cross the Plains to the California Gold Fields. San Francisco:
     William P. Wreden, 1968.
     pp. 55, illus.   540 copies
This book is highlighted by some unusual and unique illustrations
which accompany the brief but interesting narrative of Francl as he
journeyed from Wisconsin to the Coast. It was originally published in
Bratrsky" Vestni'k, a Bohemian monthly, in 1928. This original, un-
translated version usually sells in the $200.00 to $400.00 range.
     Ref.: none

163. [1854] **Franklin, John Benjamin**   1st: dd, 2nd: d, 3rd: b-c
     Horrors of Mormonism: Being a Lecture Delivered by John Ben-
     jamin Franklin . . . London: J. Appold, 1858.
     pp. 16
     2nd. ed.: *The Mysteries and the Crimes of Mormonism* . . .
        Revised by the author, with additions. London:
        C. Elliot, pp. 16

3rd. ed.: A Cheap Trip to the city of the Mormons. . . .
    Ipswich: J. Scroggins, pp. 32

anr. ed.: One Year at the Great Salt Lake City: or a Voice
    from the Utah Pandemonium. . . . Manchester: John
    Heywood, pp. 48

Franklin was an apostate and one-time manager of the Mormon printing office in Salt Lake City. He tells of his overland journey in 1854,
beginning in St. Louis and culminating in California a year later.
    Ref.: WC-299b

164. [1842] **Fremont, John C.**   bbb
    A Report on the Exploration . . . between the Missouri River and
    the Rocky Mountains . . . U.S. 27th Congress, 3rd Session,
    Senate Document 243, (Serial 416). Washington, 1843.
    pp. 207, map, 6 plates   map size, 22.5 × 14 cms.)

This is the report of Fremont's first expedition along the Oregon Trail.
This expedition veered north from the trail in western Wyoming and
climaxed in the Wind River Mountains, one of which Fremont climbed
and is now named for him.
    Ref.: G1437, H-F371, WC-95

165. [1842] **Fremont, John C.**   Sen: ccc, H.R.: c-cc, 1847: d
    Report of the Exploring Expedition to the Rocky Mountains in the
    Year 1842, and to Oregon and North California in the Years 1843–
    '44 . . . U.S. 28th Congress, 2nd Session, Senate Document
    174, (Serial 461). Washington, 1845.
    pp. 693, 22 plates, 5 maps (one is an f-map in pocket, size
    22.5 × 14.5 cms.)
    H.R. ed.: (ptd. for House of Reps.) same imprint and date,
            1847 ed.: 1847, Syracuse, pp. 427, large map by
            Rufus Sage, 2 plates
    pp. 583 (scientific data omitted)

Contains Fremont's first two narratives in which he traveled the Oregon Trail visiting Ft. Laramie, the Great Salt Lake, Ft. Hall, and
the Dalles. Certainly a cornerstone book on early exploration of the
West as well as early travelers on the Overland Trail.
    Ref.: E-p. 62, G-1436, H-F370, WC-115, Z-39

166. [1850] **Frink, Margaret A.**   ccc
    Journal of the Adventures of a Party of California Gold-seekers
    under the Guidance of Mr. Ledyard Frink during a Journey across
    the Plains from Martinsville, Indiana, to Sacramento . . March
    30, 1850 to September 7, 1850 . . . (Oakland: pvt. ptg., 1897).
    pp. 131, 2 ports.   50 copies ptd.

This very rare book tells of the trip as seen through the eyes of a woman. The toughest part was the strenuous crossing of the desert areas of Nevada. In their 1958 auction of the collection of Dr. Lester E. Bauer, the Park-Bernet Galleries could locate only two copies previously offered for sale in the U.S. (The auction copy sold for $140.00.)

        Ref.: C-p. 225, G-1445, H-F388, P-644

167. [1852] **Frizzel, Lodisa**   aaa
                Across the Plains to California in 1852 from the Little Wabash River in Illinois to the Pacific Springs of Wyoming. Edited by Hugo Paltsits. New York, 1915.
                pp. 30, 4 plates, wraps

Lodisa made entries in the journal only until she reached Fremont County, Wyoming. She used her trail notes to write the story while snowbound in the Sierras. She later reached California safely.

        Ref.: C-p. 225, G-1446, H-F3824 (1954 ed.)

168. [1860] **Fuller, Mrs. Emeline L.**   1st: c, rpt.: aa
                Left by the Indians, or Rapine, Massacre and Cannibalism on the Overland Trail in 1860. (Mt. Vernon, Iowa: Hawk-eye Steam Print, 1892).
                pp. 41, ports., wraps
                rpt.: 1936, New York, 200 copies

This is the only account by a survivor of the extreme hardships suffered by the Utter-Myers Overland Train. All but fifteen died, some from the Indian attack on the encircled wagons, some from privations. Howes says it equals the Donner tragedy, as it also involves cannibalism. The scene is the Snake River in Idaho.

        Ref.: G-1461, H-F407

169. [1864] **Fulton, Arabella**   aa
                Tales of the Trail. Montreal: pvt. ptg., 1965.
                pp. 378, illus.

A crudely printed and bound account of Arabella Fulton's overland trip to Idaho. Also included is her telling of a later trip by wagon to Texas, and her return journey.

        Ref.: none

170. [1847] **Gardner, Archibald**   a
                Life of Archibald Gardner, Utah Pioneer of 1847. Edited by Delila Gardner Hughes. Draper, Utah: Review and Preview Pub., 1970.
                pp. 232

Upon his arrival in Utah, Gardner erected the area's first sawmill. He was also responsible for one of the first flour mills in Utah. And he tells of going to the aid of the stranded handcart companies of 1856.
Ref.: none

171.   [1846]   **Garrison, Abraham Ellison**   aa
                Life and Labor of Rev. A. E. Garrison. Forty Years in Oregon.
                Seven Months on the Plains . . . N. p., pvt. ptg., 1943.
                pp. 130, wraps   207 copies
An interesting account of Garrison's trip across the plains. Accompanied by Robert Lancefield and John D. Wood, Garrison left Weston, Mo., on the fifth of May. After reaching Ft. Hall he traveled to Oregon by way of the Applegate route. This was originally written in 1887.
Ref.: none

172.   [1847]   **(Geer, Theodore T.)**   aa
                Fifty Years in Oregon. New York: Neale Pub., 1912.
                pp. 536, frontis, ports., plates
On pages 132 to 149 is quoted the overland diary of Mrs. Elizabeth Smith, who crossed the plains in 1847. She was the author's stepmother.
Ref.: none

173.   [1849]   **Geiger, Vincent Eply and Wakeman Bryarly**   aa
                Trail to California: The Overland Journal of Vincent Geiger and
                Wakeman Bryarly. Edited by David Morris Potter. New Haven: Yale University Press, 1945.
                pp. 266, maps, charts
Geiger and Bryarly were members of the Charleston Company. This day-by-day telling of their journey is one of the most desired narratives of those interested in contemporary views of the epic. Well written and informative, it is an important addition to the overland story.
Ref.: P-668, W-80

174.   [1850]   **(A) Georgian**   ccc
                The Life of the Emigrant: Great Salt Lake City and Mormonism
                at Home. By a Georgian. Milledgeville: pvt. ptd., 1854.
                pp. 64, wraps
The "Georgian" traveled with the Mormons from Council Bluffs to Salt Lake City, staying with them about a year. Never converted, he nonetheless devotes much of this book to his feelings and observations while among them. A rare book.
Ref.: WC-239c

175. [1850] **Gibbs, Mifflin W.**   b
      Shadow and Light. An Autobiography of Mifflin W. Gibbs. Wash-
      ington, 1902.
      pp. 372
Gibbs, an educated black, tells of his going overland to California in
1850. Much of the book concerns his later experiences in California
and British Columbia. A scarce book.
      Ref.: C-p. 849, H-G153

176. [1849] **Gibson, J. Watt**   bbb
      Recollections of a Pioneer. (St. Joseph, Mo., 1912).
      pp. 216, port.
Gibson made his first of three overland trips in 1849 and here relates
experiences and adventures in the land of gold mining. He returned
to Missouri in 1851, and then returned to California in 1852, driving
cattle along the way. Gibson made another cattle driving trip in 1854.
He went to Salt Lake City in 1865 and Montana in 1866. Quite an
adventurer and quite engaging reading.
      Ref.: C-p. 235, G-1546, H-G154

177. [1850] **Gill, William**   bb
      *California Letters of William Gill Written in 1850 to His Wife
      Harriet Tarleton in Kentucky.* Edited by Eva Turner Clark. New
      York: Downs Printing Co., 1922.
      pp. 43, f-map, plates, wraps (hand-tied)   100 copies
The letters were written by Gill after he reached Sacramento. His
mining efforts failed, and he often asked for money to be sent him.
In 1852 he returned home, but less than a year later he was again
going overland to Sierra Valley in California. Included here is Harriet's
diary of brief notes taken along the way. A short history of the family
is also included.
      Ref.: C-p. 237, H-G171

178. [1852] **Gillette, Martha Hill**   a
      *Overland to Oregon and in the Indian Wars of 1853; With an
      account of Earlier Life in Rural Tennessee.* Ashland: Lewis Os-
      bourne, 1971.
      pp. 80, illus., large f-map laid in   650 copies
The family began their long trip to Oregon in Tennessee and actually
made the crossing in 1852. Martha's journal includes much on her
early life before the trip and some of the later experiences such as
being caught up in the Rogue River Indian Wars, and of the special
attention given her and her sister as the only unmarried females in

Rogue River Valley. The details of the crossing are brief, sketchy, and done from memory. Nevertheless, she records many detailed facets of early pioneer life.

Ref.: none

179. [1843] **Gilpin, William**   aaa
      History of the Life of William Gilpin. San Francisco, 1889.
      pp. 62, port., map

Gilpin, who later became one of Colorado's most noted figures, gives a brief accounting of his travels overland to Oregon in 1843.

Ref.: H-G193

180. [1850] **Given, Abraham**   bbb
      Overland Trip to California in 1850. Frankfort, Ind., (ca. 1900).
      pp. 24, wraps

Given's slim pamphlet is quite rare. No record of sale for it over the past decade was found.

Ref.: C-p. 849, G-1570, H-G199

181. [1849] **Goldsmith, Oliver**   ccc
      Overland in Forty-nine. The Recollections of a Wolverine Ranger after a Lapse of Forty-seven Years. Detroit, Mich.: Published by the Author, 1896.
      pp. 148

This book is quite rare as it was printed exclusively for family and friends. Goldsmith's book is a good supplement to the letters of James Pratt. (Pratt's position as the Wolverine Ranger's chronicler is well documented in *The World Rushed In* by J. S. Holliday. Entry #231). The company of sixty-two Wolverine Rangers went over South Pass and later took Lassen's cutoff. See also the entry for "Wolverine Rangers."

Ref.: C-p. 241, G1581, H-G228, W-83

182. [1853] **Goltra, Elizabeth Julia**   a
      Journal Kept by Mrs. E. J. Goltra of Her Travels across the Plains in 1853. Eugene, Oreg.: Lane County Historical Society, 1970.
      pp. 30, wraps, ptd. on rectos only

The young Elizabeth, just twenty-two when making the journey, kept this diary with the idea of sending back reliable data, concerning all facets of the trip, to those eyeing a future move for themselves. It is a pleasing, if somewhat colorless, effort.

Ref.: none

183. [1849] **Goughnour, Emanuel** dd
Across the Plains in "49." Libertyville or Ottumwa, Iowa, (1910–11).
pp. 54, port., 1 plate
Goughnour traveled overland by way of Ft. Laramie and South Pass. The dimensions of the book are 16.6 × 10.9 cm. Reportedly only six copies of this book were printed for the six Goughnour children.
Ref.: C-p. 850, G-1601, H-G271

184. [1845] **Goulder, W. A.** b
Reminiscences. Incidents in the Life of a Pioneer in Oregon and Idaho. Boise: pvt. ptg., 1909.
pp. 376, frontis
Goulder traveled up the Missouri with Benton and Robidoux in 1844. In 1845 he went overland to Oregon, possibly with the Tethrow train. Upon reaching the Boise Valley his group was induced into taking Meek's cutoff to the Dalles, suffering many difficulties and hardships during the effort. Later he tells of mining experiences in Oregon and the Idaho diggings. (*See* 114, 206, 458.)
Ref.: G-1603, H-G277

185. [1857] **Gove, Capt. Jesse A.** L. P. Ed.: bb, 1st: aaa
The Utah Expedition 1857–58. Concord, N.H.: Historical Society, 1928.
pp. 442, 5 plates
Long Paper ed.: same, 50 copies only
Gove was a member of the expedition sent over the Trail to Salt Lake to keep order among the rebellious Mormons. These letters tell of his trip and experiences along the overland route. They are also considered a primary source for the history of the Mormon war.
Ref.: G-1604, H-G279

186. [1852] **Gowdy, Mrs. John T.** aa
Crossing the Plains, Personal Recollections of the Journey to Oregon in 1852, by Mrs. J. T. Gowdy of McMinnville. (Dayton, Oreg., 1906)
pp. 15
A very scarce item. Typical of so many of the later day reminiscences by elderly prisoners desiring to leave some record of their unforgettable experiences, brief as they may be, in conquering the plains.
Ref.: none

187. [1849]   **Graham, Martha Morgan**   1st: ccc, rpt.: cc
      The Polygamist's Victim; or, the Life Experiences of Its Author
      during a Six-Years Residence among the Mormon Saints . . . San
      Francisco: Women's Union Printing, 1872.
      pp. 72
      rpt.: *An Interesting Life History . . .* , 1875, S.F, pp. 67
A rare book by the author of an earlier and even rarer account: *A Trip*
Across the Plains in . . . 1849 . . . (see 337). This book also contains
information about her 1849–1850 journey.
          Ref.: C-p. 245, G-1610, H-G289

188. [1849]   **Gray, Charles Glass**   a
      Off at Sunrise: The Overland Journal of Charles Glass Gray.
      Edited by Thomas D. Clark. San Marino: Huntington Library
      (1976)
      pp. 182, illus., map
Since this excellent overland narrative has been only recently published it makes one wonder how many other manuscripts of this level
of interest might be forthcoming. Gray's intelligent narrative gives a
closer hint into the amount of never ending jockeying for position
that went on among the many competitive trains. Gray speaks of rising
at three and four o'clock in order that their train ". . . beat the long
lines of trains who have passed us." One of the most captivating
journals.
          Ref.: none

189. [1859]   **Greely, Horace**   b
      An Overland Journey, from New York to San Francisco, in the
      Summer of 1859. New York: C. M. Saxton, Barker and Co.,
      1860.
      pp. 386
Greely decided to take his own advice to "go west . . ." and this is
his narrative over the Overland Trail. A noteworthy book is the result,
by a well known nineteenth-century figure. Even though his travel by
stage wasn't the equivalent of the emigrant experience, it is interesting
to note the progress of "civilization" by 1859.
          Ref.: C-p. 247, G-1635, H-G355, P-723, WC-359

190. [1852]   **Green, Jay**   a
      Diary of Jay Green. Covering the Period May 1, 1852 to July
      27, 1852 during the Crossing of the Plains and Mountains in a
      Journey from Duncan's Ferry, Mo. to Hangtown . . . Edited by
      Merrell Kitchen. Stockton, Calif., 1955.
      pp. 20, illus., wraps

Green wasted no time in covering the distance between the Missouri River and Hangtown (Placerville), covering distances of thirty to forty, and at one time sixty-three miles per day. One wonders how he did it, yet Green says next to nothing about his use of animals or equipment. The high spot of this overly dry diary is his description of the trial and execution, prairie style, of one man for the murder of another. This is the fifth publication of the San Joaquin Pioneer and Historical Society.

> Ref.: none

191.   [1847]   **(Green, Nelson Winch)**   ccc
Fifteen Years Among the Mormons. Being the Narrative of Mrs. Mary Ettie V. Smith . . . a Sister of One of the Mormon High Priests . . . and Long in the Confidence of the "Prophet" Brigham Young . . . New York: Scribner, 1858.
pp. 388, frontis
rpt.: 1858, N.Y., H. Dayton, Nassau St.
     1859, N.Y., same
     1859, N.Y., H. Dayton, Howard St.
     1860, N.Y., same

Mary Ettie was one of the Mormons who left Nauvoo in 1846 for the journey westward. However, in 1856, she returned after having personality differences with those at Salt Lake City.

> Ref.: G-1640, WC-300

192.   [1855]   **Guerin, Mrs. E. J.**   1st: dd, rpt.: a
Mountain Charlie, or the Adventures of Mrs. E. J. Guerin, Who was Thirteen Years in Male Attire. Dubuque: Published for the Author, 1861.
pp. 45, wraps
rpt.: 1968, Norman, pp. 112

In the introduction to the University of Oklahoma reprint, editors Fred W. Mazzulla and William Kostka report that by 1853, when Charles L. Camp prepared the third edition of *The Plains and the Rockies*, only one copy of the first printing of this book was reported in existence. That copy was sold to Everett L. DeGolyer Jr., of Dallas, by Fred Rosenstock, and is the copy used for the reprint edition. Mrs. Guerin includes excerpts from her 1855 overland diary to furnish the reader with highlights of her journey to the Sacramento Valley.

> Ref.: H-G453, WC-374a

193. [1849] **(Hafen, Leroy R. and Ann W.)** a
      *Journals, Diaries and Letters, Being a Supplement to Volume
      2 . . .* (Vol. 15 of Far West and Rockies Series). Glendale:
      Arthur H. Clark Co., 1956.
      pp. 124, 2 ports. (also includes series index)
   Fourteen additional forty-niner accounts are provided in the first 124
   pages of this volume. All are again concerned with the "Mormon Trail"
   route from Utah to California. Included are the documents of Judge
   H. S. Brown, Dr. C. N. Ormsby, Mr. Shearer, Leonard Babcock,
   Joseph P. Hamelin, three new sources concerning the Huffaker train,
   and others.
      Ref.: none

194. [1849] **(Hafen, Leroy R. and Ann W.)** aa
      Journals of the Forty-niners. (Vol. 2, Far West and Rockies
      Series). Glendale: Arthur H. Clark Co., 1954.
      pp. 333, illus.
   Contains diaries and contemporary records of Sheldon Young, James
   S. Brown, Jacob Y. Stover, Charles C. Rich, Addison Pratt, Howard
   Egan, Henry W. Bigler, plus a number of others. Concerns, for the
   most part, those accounts that have bearing, or add color, to the
   Jayhawker group that gave Death Valley its notoriety and name. Most
   of the travelers came by way of South Pass; a few, such as Addison
   Pratt, took other routes. Interesting reading, and nicely printed by
   the Clark Co.
      Ref.: E-p. 68

195. [1856] **(Hafen, Leroy R. and Ann W.)** aa
      *Handcarts to Zion; the Story of a Unique Western Migration,
      1856–1860, with Contemporary Journals, Accounts, Reports,
      and Rosters . . .* Glendale: Arthur H. Clark Co., 1960.
      pp. 328, map, frontis, 10 illus.
   Also issued as Vol. XIV of "The Far West and Rockies" series. The
   Hafens tell of the ten Handcart Companies, including contemporary
   accounts by those involved, and even information on the handcarts
   themselves. Another nicely printed book from the Arthur H. Clark
   Co.
      Ref.: none

196. [1860] **Hafen, Mary Ann (Stucki)** aaa
      *Recollections of a Handcart Pioneer of 1860 with Some Account
      of Frontier Life in Utah and Nevada.* Denver: pvt. ptg., 1938.
      pp. 117, photos, frontis

The niece of Utah pioneer John Stucki, Mary Ann was the mother
of the well known historian Leroy Hafen. She crossed the plains with
her family, having come all the way from Switzerland. All handcart
users had to walk, and she says of her mother, "By this time mother's
feet were so swollen that she could not wear shoes, but had to wrap
her feet with cloth." Appendix B is a family record. This is a tough
book to find.

> Ref.: P-753

197.   [1849]   **Hale, Israel F.**   aa
> *Diary of Trip to California in 1849.* San Francisco: Society of
> California Pioneers Quarterly, 1925.
>
> pp. 72, wraps

Hale wrote this for his family and thus it is a fairly detailed account.
He was one of those who made the intriguing and usually quite difficult
journey westward from the Humboldt across the Black Rock Desert.
The route was sometimes called the "death route" but was commonly
known as Lassen's cutoff. A few years later it was virtually abandoned.

> Ref.: none

198.   [1849]   **Hale, John**   1st: dd, rpt.: b
> *California As It Is; Being a Description of a Tour by the Overland
> Route and South Pass of the Rocky Mountains.* Rochester: Printed
> for the Author, by W. Heughes, Main Street, 1851.
>
> pp. 40, wraps
>
> rpt.: 1954, San Francisco, Grabhorn Press, 150 copies

Hale speaks disparagingly of the emigration to California. After reaching California by way of Lassen's cutoff, he stayed just a year before
returning home. One of the rarest of the overland narratives. Size of
the book is 20 × 11.5 cm., and there are only a few known existing
copies.

> Ref.: C-p. 852, G-1716, H-H31, WC-198a

199.   [1864]   **Hall, Edward H.**   cc
> *The Great West: Travelers', miners', and emigrants' Guide and
> Handbook to the States of California and Oregon. . .* New York:
> Tribune Office, 1864.
>
> pp. 89, map (12.5 × 35 cms.), wraps

Hall's guide to the ". . . Western, Northwestern, and the Pacific States
and Territories" was issued a year after this. Wagner-Camp-Becker calls
this guidebook a "scissors-and-paste compilation. . . ."

> Ref.: C-p. 258, G-1724, H-H55, WC-400

200. [1849] **Hall, John B.**   d
      An Account of California and the Wonderful Gold Regions . . .
      with a Description of the Different Routes to California . . . Bos-
      ton: J. B. Hall (1849).

          pp. 32 (unnumbered), maps (map size 23 × 11 cms.), wraps
This thin book is quite rare, as are most of the early overland guides.
          Ref.: WC-167f

201. [1849] **Hall, Thomas Wakeman**   bb
      Recollections of a Grandfather. Edited by Elizebeth (Hall) Ball.
      Oak Park, Ill., 1895.

          pp. 48
Hall recalls his journey to California during the gold rush. He later
returned home to Wisconsin with a fair amount of gold. This book
was issued in a very small edition and is seldom seen for sale.
          Ref.: C-p. 259, G-1743, H-H87

202. [1850] **Hamblin, Jacob**   b
      Jacob Hamblin, a Narrative of His Personal Experience, as a
      Frontiersman, Missionary to the Indians and Explorer . . . Per-
      ilous Situations and Remarkable Escapes. Fifth book of Faith-
      Promoting Series . . . Salt Lake City: Juvenile Instructor Of-
      fice, 1881.

          pp. 140 and 4 (ads.)
          2nd ed.: 1909, pp. 151
          rpt.:   1969, pp. 149
This is Hamblin's story as told to Little. He is perhaps the best known
Mormon frontiersman and was involved with many of the early-day
Utah events. Mention is made of work with the Indians, the Mountain
Meadows Massacre, his explorations, and more.
          Ref.: G-2511, H-L383, P-1157

203. [1857] **Hamilton, Henry S.**   aa
      Reminiscences of a Veteran. Concord, N.H.: Republican Press,
      1897.

          pp. 180, port., plates
Hamilton served in the Army for a time under Capt. Jesse Gove. His
important narrative details his adventures at Fort Snelling, at Fort
Ridgely, and his expedition across the plains in 1857. He speaks of
the Mormon War and other campaigns during the years 1857–60, and
of some of the resulting hardships.
          Ref.: G-1753

204.   [1853]   **Hamilton, Mrs. S. Watson**   aaa-cc
       *A Pioneer of "Fifty-three." (Rhyming account of a trip from Iowa,
       to Oregon)*. Albany, Oreg., 1905.
           pp. 139, port.
A very rare account according to Howes, whose information states
that only three copies survived the burning of Mrs. Hamilton's home
just after they had been delivered from the printers. This may be an
underestimate, as two copies were offered for sale in 1982. Prices asked
were $100.00 and $600.00. As the title indicates, it is a somewhat
detailed version of her trip written in rhyme, probably containing
more than a sprinkling of fiction.
           Ref.: H-H135

205.   [1849]   **Hamilton, W. T.**   b
       My Sixty Years on the Plains. New York: Forest and Stream,
       1905.
           pp. 244, frontis port., 8 illus. by Charles M. Russell
Hamilton, a trapper, and some cronies, decided to try their luck in
the mines around Sacramento after talking to many of those on the
Oregon Trail who spoke highly of the easy fortunes to be had. They
arrived in Hangtown on July 3rd, and Hamilton surmised that because
of the number of those already mining, thousands must have come by
boat. This unsuccessful venture, one of the many episodes included
in this book, lasted until 1853. Very little is said about his overland
experiences.
           Ref.: G-1759, H-H139

206.   [1845]   **Hancock, Samuel**   L. P. Ed.: b, 1st ed.: aa-aaa
       The Narrative of Samuel Hancock, 1845–1860. New York: R.
       M. McBride & Co., 1927.
           pp. 240, reproduction of Mitchell map of Oregon Trail 1846
A limited edition of 65 copies was done on long paper. This is perhaps
the best firsthand account of the party led by Stephen Meek during
which he sought, disastrously, to reach Oregon by an unproven cutoff.
In the same party were William A. Goulder, Sarah Cummins, and
Sol. Tethrow. Overall, this is an excellent narrative. The introduction
is by Arthur D. Smith.
           Ref.: C-p. 853

207.   [1853]   **Handsaker, Samuel**   bb
       Pioneer Life. Eugene, Oreg., 1908.
           pp. 104, 3 plates, 2 facs.
Handsaker, born in England, kept a day-by-day diary of his 1853 trek
to Oregon. His comments and observations give color to his writings.

A scarce book seldom seen for sale. See also *Autobiography, Diary, and Reminiscences of Samuel Handsaker,* published by the Lane County Pioneer Historical Society (Eugene, 1965).

Ref.: H-H156

208. [1849] **(Hannon, Jessie Gould, Ed.)**   a
The Boston-Newton Company Venture from Massachusetts to California in 1849. Lincoln: University of Nebraska Press, (1969).
pp. 224, e-maps, illus.

From the preface: "This volume brings together companion diaries kept by Charles Gould [the editor's grandfather], and Jackson Staples, members of the Boston-Newton Joint Stock Association during the Company's overland journey from Boston to Sutter's Fort. . . ." Gould's diary is printed here for the first time. However, a sixty-three page typescript was offered for sale (N. p., N. d.) and the number of such in existence is not known. The Staples journal previously appeared in *The California Historical Quarterly.*

Ref.: none

209. [1849] **Hanson, D. M.**   bb
Recollections of Honorable D. M. Hanson Crossing the Plains in '49 Written in 1919 (Being in his 79th year). N. p., N. d. (circa 1919)
pp. (16), wraps

Hanson tells of nearly starving in the Sierra Mountains in winter, and of traveling through the mining towns and camps the following spring. As he prepared to leave Charleston, Illinois to begin his overland trip in April of 1849 his father provided him with an abundance of potent "medicine" to ward off cholera. A very scarce book.

Ref.: none

210. [1843] **(Hardeman, Nicholas Perkins)**   a
Wilderness Calling. Knoxville: University of Tennessee, 1977.
pp. 357, map, illus.

Tells the history of the Hardeman family, including Peter Hardeman Burnett who crossed the plains in 1843 (*see* 66).

Ref.: none

211. [1846] **Harlan, Jacob W.**   bb
California, 1846 to 1888. San Francisco: The Bancroft Co., 1888.
pp. 242, port.

Harlan, a member of the Boggs-Moran party, went as far as Ft. Bridger with the Donner party where, by luck, he opted for the Fort Hall route, leaving the Donner group to attempt the cutoff that resulted in the delays that cost so many lives. He became an active participant in the California revolution, and, in 1853, made his second overland crossing bringing with him 118 cattle.

Ref.: C-p. 264, G-1783, H-H198, W-90

212. [1847]   **Harmon, Appleton Milo**   aa
Journals; Participant in Mormon Exodus from Illinois and Early Settlement of Utah . . . Edited by Maybelle Harmon Anderson. N. p., N. d. (1946, Berkeley), pvt. ptg.
pp. 208, illus., title page in color
also: 1946, Glendale, Arthur H. Clark Co., pp. 208
Harmon, an inventor, helped design the first roadmeter, the forerunner of the speedometer. He also tells of his ferrying operation at the Platte River Ferry, and of his later adventures traveling to Europe. His simple telling of the Mormon trek is a good one.

Ref.: none

213. [1851]   **Harris, Sarah Hollister**   c
An Unwritten Chapter of Salt Lake 1851–1901. New York: pvt. ptg., 1901.
pp. 89
Only a few copies were printed for the family. Sarah was the wife of Broughton D. Harris, first Secretary and Treasurer of the Territory. Her diary includes a detailed record of the overland trip to Salt Lake in 1851. Also of interest, a chapter on Salt Lake entitled "Forty Years Later."

Ref.: G-1795, H-H231

214. [1864]   **Harter, George**   aa
Crossing the Plains; an Account of the George Harter Family's Trip from Cass County, Michigan to Marysville, California in 1864 . . . Sacramento (circa 1957)
23 leaves
Transcribed by Doris Harter Chase from her grandfather's diary. Scarce.

Ref.: none

215. [1842]   **Hastings, Lansford Warren**   1st: ddd, 2nd ed.: dd,
                                                1932 ed.: aa
The Emigrants Guide to Oregon and California, Containing Scenes and Incidents of a Party of Oregon Emigrants; A Description of Oregon; Scenes and Incidents of a Party of California Emigrants;

and a Description of California . . . Cincinnati: George Con-
clin, Pub., 1845.

rpt.: A second ed. was published in Cincinnati in 1845 and
an enlarged ed. in 1847, followed by a number of other
printings (including 1932, Princeton University).

The infamous Hastings joined Elijah White's party at Elm Grove,
Kansas. He soon took charge because of the party's dissatisfaction with
White's leadership. Because of the difficulties encountered by almost
all who took Hasting's cutoff, including the Donner Party, this is
probably the most controversial of all guidebooks, and one of the most
important early books concerning overland travel. Less than a dozen
copies of the first printing are known to exist.

Ref.: G-1815, H-H288, WC-116, Z-41

216. [1849] **Haun, Catherine**   a
Women's Diaries of the Westward Journey. Edited by Lillian
Schlissel. New York: Schocken, (1982).

pp. 262, frontis, map, illus.

This reminiscent account, told by Mrs. Haun to her daughter in later
years, occupies pages 165 to 185 of this engaging book. As a young
bride, Mrs. Haun traveled with her husband from Iowa to Sacramento.

Ref.: none

217. [1860] **Hawkins, Thomas Samuel**   b
Some Recollections of a Busy Life. San Francisco: pvt. ptg.,
1913.

pp. 161, frontis   300 copies ptd.

A scarce book concerning Hawkins's life in Missouri, his trip overland,
and life in California.

Ref.: C-p. 271, H-H321

218. [1850] **Hayden, Mary J.**   d
Pioneer Days. San Jose: Murgotten Press, 1915.

pp. 49, frontis, wraps (tied)

Howes says this "tells of her 1850 overland trip to Oregon, Indian
wars, etc." It is reported that only a few copies were printed for the
family. The Haydens were members of the Wisconsin Blues, of which
John Steele was also a member, and which left Kanesville, Iowa on
the tenth of May. Settling near Vancouver Barracks, she gives a stirring
view of pioneer life. Considered by some dealers of Americana as one
of the rarest of all overland narratives.

Ref.: H-H341

219.   [1849]   **Hayes, Benjamin**   aaa
       *Pioneer Notes from the Diaries of Judge Benjamin Hayes 1849–
       1875.* Los Angeles: pvt. ptg., 1929.
       pp. 307, frontis, illus.
Part of Hayes's diary is an account of a trip overland from Liberty,
Missouri to California. Most of the book covers his experiences in
southern California. Reportedly issued in a small edition.
       Ref.: none

220.   [1850]   **(Hayes, Charles W., Ed.)**   bbb
       George Edward Hayes, a Memorial. Buffalo, 1882.
       pp. 174, port.
Described by Howes as ". . . an eventful trip across the plains in 1850."
This book was possibly a family project issued in a small quantity only,
as today it is quite difficult to locate a copy.
       Ref.: H-H343

221.   [1846]   **Hecox, Margaret M.**   a
       *California Caravan. The 1846 Overland Trail Memoir of Mar-
       garet M. Hecox.* Edited by Richard Dillon. San Jose, 1966.
       pp. 70, photos, illus.   675 copies
An interesting reckoning of a journey from St. Joseph to California.
       Ref.: none

222.   [1862]   **Hewitt, Randall H.**   1st: dd, 2nd ed.: cc, 3rd ed.: bb
       *Notes by the Way: Memoranda of a Journey across the Plains,
       from Dundee, Ill., to Olympia, W. T., May 7, to November 3,
       1862.* Olympia: Office of Washington Standard, 1863.
       pp. 58, wraps
       2nd ed.: 1872, Olympia
       3rd ed.: (1906), *Across the Plains and Over the Divide,* pp.
          521, port.
The 2nd ed. was reprinted in Seattle in 1955. The 3rd ed., along
with being greatly enlarged, has 58 plates, some copies having 59,
with a plate titled "Variegated" facing p. 230. The first two editions
are rare; the third scarce. This is a detailed overland narrative to the
Northwest part of the nation via South Pass. Hewitt's narrative is a
good example of the nation's early pathfinders. The author went from
Ft. Laramie by way of the Lander cutoff through what is now Wyoming,
and over the Mullan Road to the Columbia. Hewitt's journal is one
of the few printed of an 1862 crossing. Only a half-dozen or so copies
of the first edition exist in complete form.
       Ref.: G-1876, H-H457, WC-391

223. [1850] **Heywood, Martha Spence** a
Not by Bread Alone. The Journal of Martha Spence Haywood.
Edited by Juanita Brooks. Salt Lake City: Utah State Historical Society, 1978.
pp. 141, frontis port., illus.
Martha's overland diary to Salt Lake composes the first three chapters,
with incidents of Mormon life comprising the rest. She tells of the
problems of the journey, including a multitude of those involving her
health. This is a significant diary of Mormon life in the 1800s. Nicely
printed.
Ref.: none

224. [1852] **Hickman, Richard Owen** a
An Overland Journey to California in 1852. Edited by Catherine
White. Missoula: University of Montana Press, 1929.
pp. 21, wraps
This short narrative is reprinted from *Frontier Magazine.* It gives some
insight into the trading posts, which, by 1852, were already established
along the Humboldt River.
Ref.: C-p. 278, P-841

225. [1849] **Hickman, William A.** aaa
*Brigham's Destroying Angel: Being the Life, Confession, and Star-
tling Disclosures of the Notorious Bill Hickman, the Danite Chief
of Utah* . . . New York: George A. Crofutt, 1872.
pp. 219, illus.
rpt.: 1904, Salt Lake City, pp. 221, port., illus.
Most of the book revolves around the deeds and misdeeds of Hickman.
His crossing of the plains is relegated to secondary importance.
Ref.: G-1879, H-H465

226. [1849] **Hill, Jasper S.** aa
*The Letters of a Young Miner Covering the Adventures of Jasper
S. Hill during the California Gold Rush 1849–1852.* Edited by
Doyce B. Nunis Jr. San Francisco, 1964.
pp. 111, f-map, illus. 475 copies
Printed very nicely by John Howell. The overland portion occupies
only a few pages since most of the book pertains to his experiences
as a miner.
Ref.: none

227. [1849] **(Hinckley, Ted, Ed.)**   a
      *Overland from St. Louis to the California Gold Field in 1849;
      the Diary of Joseph Waring Berrien.* N. p., 1960.
      pp. 80
Berrien gives the account of his trip that began on March 31st and
concluded on the 15th of August. This pamphlet is a separate printing
of a diary that appeared in the *Indiana Magazine of History.*
      Ref.: none

228. [1849] **Hindman, David**   c
      The Way to My Golden Wedding. St. Joseph, Mo.: American
      Printing Co.
      pp. 200, 2 plates
Hindman tells of his trip to Illinois in 1846, and then on to California
in 1849. Graff says "Pages 10–67 give a splendid description of overland travel." Hindman's party traveled by way of Hudspeth's cutoff to
the Humboldt and on to Weaverville losing only two oxen along the
way. This book sold for $240.00 in the Streeter auction.
      Ref.: G-1895, H-H501

229. [1849] **Hinman, Charles G.**   aa
      "A Pretty Fair View of the Eliphent" (sic) Edited by Colton
      Storm. Chicago, Ill.: Gordon Martin, 1960.
      pp. 45 (limitation notice on p. 47), frontis, 200 copies (ptd.
      for Everett D. Graff)
Ten letters which Hinman wrote to his wife comprise this narrative.
It appears he returned east after failing to find any great fortune in
the mines. Attractively printed.
      Ref.: G-1901

230. [1852] **(Hixon, Adrietta A.)**   aa
      *On to Oregon; a True Story of a Young Girl's Journey into the
      West.* (Weiser, Idaho, 1947).
      pp. 48, ports., heavy wraps   100 copies
The overland story of Mary Ellen Todd, from Arkansas to Oregon in
1852. Once in the territory she married John Applegate. Hers is a
vividly told narrative, and includes a clash with the Indians and a
rescue by the men of Joab Powell's train. These reminiscences were
told to, and written by, Mrs. Applegate's daughter. Somewhat difficult
to find.
      Ref.: none

231. [1849] **(Holliday, J. S.)**   a
      The World Rushed In. New York: Simon and Shuster (1981).
      pp. 559, e-maps, maps, photos, illus.
Mr. Holliday employs in excellent fashion the letters and diary of gold
seeker William Swain. Swain felt it a family duty to write a fully
detailed report of his overland trip to the diggings, his stay there and
his return home to Youngstown, N.Y. To add to the day-by-day un-
folding of Swain's adventures, letters from his brother and wife are
inserted at appropriate intervals of the diary to allow the reader a
view, not only of the trials facing Swain, but also of the strained
feelings of those left behind. For a wider scope the author utilizes
quotes from members of the Wolverine Rangers, the company Swain
was a part of, along with observances by J. G. Bruff, Oliver Goldsmith,
and other contemporaries who were just a day or so away. This book,
along with John D. Unruh's *The Plains Across* (1979, University of
Illinois), may be the two most important and relevant books concerning overland travel published in the past ten years.
      Ref.: none

232. [1845] **Holman, Woodford C.**   bb
      Twenty-four Years Residence in California and Oregon. St. Louis,
      1870.
      pp. 25, wraps
Although Holman traveled overland to Oregon in 1845, most of this
pamphlet deals with other interests.
      Ref.: H-H606

233. [1850] **(Holmes, Kenneth L., Ed.)**   a
      Covered Wagon Women. Vol. II. Glendale: Arthur H. Clark
      Co., 1983.
      pp. 294, frontis
Included here are letters and diaries written by women during their
travels west in the year 1850. The highlight of this second volume in
a projected series of ten is the reprinting of the magnetic, and quite
scarce, journal by Margaret Frink. Other 1850 diaries included are by
Sarah Davis to California; Lucena Parsons also on her way to the gold
mines, and Sophia Lois Goodridge on the Mormon Trail to Salt Lake.
Finely printed by the Clark Company.
      Ref.: none

234. [1851] **(Holmes, Kenneth L., Ed.)**   a
      Covered Wagon Women. Vol. III. Glendale: Arthur H. Clark
      Co., 1984.
      pp. 283, frontis

Volume three in this series includes the diaries or letters of six women bound for Oregon, one woman bound for Utah, and the short letter of a woman already in California. All entries are concerned with the year 1851. Those with Oregon as their destination are Harriet Talcott Buckingham; Amelia Hadley, who ironically mislabeled her diary *Journal of Travails to Oregon*; a perfunctory recording of events by Susan Amelia Cranston; a diary/letter by Lucia Loraine Williams; the short diaries of Elizabeth Wood and Eugenia Zieber; and a most colorful entry by Jean Rio Baker going to Salt Lake. This volume makes an important contribution to the scanty list of published overland accounts for the year 1851.

Ref.: none

235.   [1852]   **(Holmes, Kenneth L., Ed.)**   a
Covered Wagon Women. Vol. IV. Glendale: Arthur H. Clark Co., 1985.
pp. 295, frontis, illus.
The fourth volume of this series presents the records of six women headed for California in 1852. Included are a letter by Elizabeth Keegan; a diary by seventeen-year-old Eliza Ann McCauley; *Kentucky to California By Carriage and a Feather Bed,* by Francis Sawyer, who actually traveled most of the way embracing such comforts; a moving diary by Marriett Foster which includes an epilogue; and the skeletal reporting of Sarah Pratt.

Ref.: none

236.   [1852]   **(Holmes, Kenneth L., Ed.)**   a
Covered Wagon Women. Vol. V. Glendale: Arthur H. Clark Co., 1986.
pp. 312, illus.
Volume Five of this series contains the diaries of women headed overland to Oregon in 1852. It includes the lengthy day-by-day diary of Abigail Jane Scott, who later as Abigail Duniway (*see* 135) wrote fictionalized versions of her experiences. Polly Coon and Martha S. Read wrote short, but detailed, accounts. And Cecilia Adams and Parthenia Blank were twin sisters who, appropriately enough, combined on a diary of their journey.

Ref.: none

237.   [1841]   **Hopper, Charles**   aa
Charles Hopper and the Pilgrims of the Pacific. An 1841 California Pioneer, His Narrative and Other Documents. La Grange, Calif.: Southern Mines Press, 1981.
pp. 160, facs., illus., maps   350 copies

Hopper, a member of the Bartleson-Bidwell party, gave an oral history interview to R. T. Montgomery in 1871, but it wasn't published until 1981. Some other accounts dealing with the famous 1841 trek are also included, plus statements by James Findla, Alexander Moore, and William Alexander Trubody, all of whom made the journey in 1847.

Ref.: none

238. [1852] **Horn, Hosea B.**   1st: d, 2nd ed.: cc, 3rd.: c

Horn's Overland Guide, from the U. S. Indian Sub-agency, Council Bluffs, on the Missouri River, to the City of Sacramento . . . Containing a Table of Distances and Showing All the Rivers, Creeks, Lakes, Springs, Mountains, Hills, Camping-places, and Other Prominent Objects. . . . New York: J. H. Colton, 1852. pp. 78, f-map (28.5 × 46.5)

2nd ed.: 1852, New York, pp. 83 (includes 18 ad. pages at end), pages 77–78 reversed

3rd ed.: (1853) New York, pp. 84 (24 ad. pages)

In the first issue, newspaper notices do not appear under "Certificates" on page five, as they do in later issues. Also, an ad. for the Council Bluffs Agency appears on page sixty-eight of the first issue. It appears on page eighty-four in later issues. This was one of the more popular handbooks of the day. Horn had traveled over the trail, with some of its cutoffs, and prepared this guide from his experiences. Some feel this guide is the best of its kind.

Ref.: G-1955, H-H641, P-890, W-105, WC-214

239. [1857] **Horton, Emily McGowan**   bbb

Our Family, with a Glimpse of Their Pioneer Life. (Salt Lake City), 1922. pp. 46

Emily also authored *My Scrapbook* (*see* 240), a later version of her family's observations going overland. As with her other work, this too is very scarce.

Ref.: none

240. [1857] **Horton, Emily McGowan**   bb

My Scrapbook. Seattle, Wash., 1927. pp. 63

The family traveled from Kansas to California in 1857. She tells about the Plains Register at Scott's Bluff and also describes some of the other trail scenes of this year. Scarce.

Ref.: none

241. [1846] **Houghton, Eliza P. Donner**   aaa
       The Expedition of the Donner Party and Its Tragic Fate. Chicago:
       A. C. McClurg, 1911.
       pp. 375, 56 illus.
Eliza was the daughter of George and Tamsen Donner and was only
three or four-years old when her historic family perished in the snow
of the Sierras. She tells of the tragedy and of later life in California.
Nicely reprinted by the Arthur H. Clark Co. in 1920.
       Ref.: C-p. 856, G-1971, P-892

242. [1850] **(Hubbard, Earle R.)**   aa
       Sparks From Many Campfires. Raymond, S. Dak., 1959.
       pages unnumbered, wraps
This contains the diary of the author's father, Chauncey D. Hubbard,
who went overland from York, Ohio to the American River in California. His group opted for taking the Hastings cutoff causing them
much difficulty. He arrived at the diggings with a small group, on foot.
This pamphlet also has a chapter on the Montana Vigilantes, and one
called "Indians." Probably printed in a small edition.
       Ref.: none

243. [1847] **Hulin, Lester**   a
       Day Book or Journal, Oregon Trail and Applegate Route, 1847.
       Eugene, Oreg.: Lane County Pioneer Historical Society, 1959.
       pp. 30, port., facs. (mounted), typescript
Besides containing a short biographical sketch of Hulin, this also
includes reproductions of the pencil sketches with which he illustrated
his diary. He entered Oregon by way of the Applegate route.
       Ref.: none

244. [1852] **Hull, Cyrus**   aa
       *A Long Road to Stony Creek: Being the Narrative of Rufus
       Burrows and Cyrus Hill, of Their Eventful Lives in the Wilderness
       West of 1848–1858.* Ashland: Lewis Osbourne, 1971.
       pp. 70, illus., e-map   650 copies
The Burrows narrative occupies most of this book (see 67). Hull's
journey is described in two letters.
       Ref.: none

245. [1847] **Hunt, George W.**   aa
       *A History of the Hunt Family, from the Norman Conquest, 1066
       A.D., to . . . Settlement in Oregon; Mining Experience in Cal-
       ifornia in 1849; Incidents of Pioneer Life.* Boston, 1890.
       pp. 79

Includes Hunt's record of an overland trip in 1847 to Oregon. This
is the same G. W. Hunt that Fred Lockley's book, *To Oregon by Ox-
team* is about.
> Ref.: H-H802

246. [1854] **Hunt, Nancy A. (Zumwalt)**   bb
> *By Ox-team to California in 1854. Personal Narrative of Nancy
> A. Hunt.* Edited by Rockwell D. Hunt (N. p., 1916).
> pp. 14, ports., plates

A scarce little book, reprinted from *The Overland Monthly,* April, 1916,
most probably in San Francisco.
> Ref.: C-p. 297

247. [1852] **Hunter, George**   1st: b, 2nd ed.: aa
> *Reminiscences of an Old Timer.* San Francisco: H. S. Crocker
> Co., 1887.
> pp. 454, frontis port., 15 plates
> 2nd ed.: 1887
> rpt.:   (with additions) 1888 and 1889, Battle Creek, Mich.,
>   pp. 508

Hunter tells of going overland by wagon train to Oregon and California. In addition, he includes chapters on mining and an account
of the Rogue River war of 1853.
> Ref.: C-p. 298, G-2018, H-H811

248. [1854] **Huntington, O. B.**   a
> *Eventful Narratives . . . Designed for the Instruction and En-
> couragment of Latter-Day Saints.* Salt Lake City: Juvenile In-
> structor Office, 1887.
> pp. 98

A book concerned with Mormon narratives, one of which is Huntington's journey to Carson Valley in 1854. Wagner-Camp-Becker
mentions Huntington, but gives no information on this book. Information can be found in Flake's *A Mormon Bibliography.*
> Ref.: none

249. [1849] **Hutchings, James Mason**   a
> *Seeking the Elephant 1849; Journal of his Overland Trek to Cal-
> ifornia.* Edited by Shirley Sargent. Glendale: Arthur H. Clark
> Co., 1980.
> pp. 212, 2 illus.   750 copies

The Hutchings book is volume XI of the *American Trail Series.* Hutchings was an early California journalist and author of *The Miner's Ten
Commandments,* and other works.
> Ref.: none

250. [1845] **(Ide, Simeon)**   1st: ccc, 2nd ed.: cc, rpt.: aa
      *A Biographical Sketch of the Life of William B. Ide; with a Minute
      and Interesting Account of One of the Largest Emigrating Com-
      panies . . . to the Pacific Coast. . . .* (Claremont, N.H.): Pub-
      lished for the subscribers, (1880).
      pp. 240   80 copies ptd.
      rpt.: *The Conquest of California*, 1944, Grabhorn Press, San
      Francisco, 500 copies
Concerning the book, Ide said: "I spent upwards of two years in its
production, set it into type myself, did all the proofreading and cor-
recting, printed it on my 'toy' printing press, attended to the making
of its plates and forms, and even to folding and gathering the sheets
ready for the binder." He was 86 years old at the time. Copies of the
book are rare, one source stating only eighty copies were printed. It
is sometimes seen in a variant binding with an extra end leaf at front
and back. It includes recollections by his daughter of the family's trip
across the plains to California in 1845, and some information on the
Bear Flag revolt of 1846 as told by W. B. Ide to his brother in 1849.
      Ref.: G-2059, H-I4, Z-45

251. [1850] **Ingalls, Eleazar S.**   dd
      *Journal of a Trip to California by the Overland Route Across the
      Plains in 1850–51.* Waukegan, Ill.: Tobey & Co., 1852.
      pp. 51 and 3 ad. pages   six or fewer copies known
A very good Overland narrative. Easy to follow and entertaining.
Ingalls tells of many episodes involving human frailties. He provides
one of the best accounts of the havoc of the 1850 overlanders in
crossing the Nevada deserts. Included is a short, amusing entry concerning a confusing crossing of the trails he calls "Fools Meadow."
Much of this journal is involved with the human events that transpired
along the trail, and less so, as with so many other diaries, with the
physical aspects of the route. Mr. Glen Adams of Ye Galleon Press
recently reprinted this rare book (Fairfield, 1979, pp. 80 and 8, illus.).
      Ref.: C-p. 303, G2106, H-I34, P-942, WC-215

252. [1854] **Ingalls, Rufus Capt.**   b
      *Reports by Captain Rufus Ingalls on the March from Fort Leav-
      enworth to Salt Lake City, and from that Place to San Francisco
      Bay.* U.S. 34th Congress, 1st Session, Senate Document 1,
      pt. 2, (Serial 811). H.R. Doc. 1, (Serial 841), Washington,
      1855.
      pp. 152–168
Ingalls gives a factual report of his overland journey under the leadership of Lt. Col. E. J. Steptoe, of whom he speaks highly. Ingalls,

after stating he greatly enjoyed his trip along the Humboldt, left Steptoe's command at Lassen's Meadows and traveled the Applegate Trail to the Rogue River area. He includes some interesting descriptions of debris on the Black Rock Desert.

Ref.: WC-256

253.   [1847]   **Ingersoll, Chester**   aa
Overland to California in 1847. Chicago: Black Cat Press, 1937.
pp. 50   350 copies
This account was originally published in the Joliet newspaper in 1847–48. Ingersoll did a reliable job of "reporting." He called Ft. Hall a "shaving shop . . . worst place for the emigrants . . . almost destitute of honesty or human feelings." The diary is formed from letters written on the trail and sent to the newspaper.

Ref.: H-139, P-943

254.   [1849]   **Isham, Giles S.**   dd
Guide to California and the Mines, and Return by the Isthmus, with a General Description of the Country, Compiled from a Journal Kept by Him in a Journey to That Country, in 1849 and 1850. New York: A. T. Houel, Printer, 1850.
pp. 32
rpt.: Fairfield, Wash., 1972
Isham concludes his somewhat bare narrative with his "advice to emigrants for California." Measurements of the 1850 printing are 14.5 by 9.5 cm. Only a few copies are known to exist.

Ref.: H-189, WC-183

255.   [1853]   **Ivins, Virginia Wilcox**   1st: c, rpt.: aaa
Pen Pictures of Early Western Days. Illustrated by W. S. Ivins. (Keokuk, Iowa), pvt. ptg., 1905.
pp. 157, plates, frontis, plates
rpt.: 1908, pp. 160, frontis, illus.
Mrs. Ivins tells of her journey with her husband to California from Iowa. Originally printed in a small private edition.

Ref.: C-p. 306, G-2168, H-193

256.   [1847]   **Jacob, Norton**   aaa
The Record of Norton Jacob. Edited by C. Edward and Ruth S. Jacob. Salt Lake City: Norton Jacob Family, 1949.
pp. 114

A scarce book. Jacob relates incidents involving Indians and buffalo. He traveled to Salt Lake City to be ". . . independent of all the power of the gentiles. . . ." His memoirs also include plural marriage and the resultant problems.

Ref.: none

257. [1852] **Jacobs, Orange**   aa
      Memoirs of Orange Jacobs Containing Many Interesting Amusing and Instructive Incidents. . . . Seattle, Wash.: Lowman & Hanford Co., 1908.
      pp. 234, frontis port.

After graduating with a law degree, Jacobs traveled west in 1852 as a member of a small group. His father said to him, "Go West, my son . . . go to Oregon—not to California—for you would amount to nothing as a miner. You will be subject to a continual alkaline bath on the plains, and this will prepare you for the renovating effects of the salubrious air of the Pacific Coast." In the copy of this book examined, pages 37–40 were out of order.

Ref.: H-J37

258. [1848] **Johnson, Benjamin Franklin**   a
      My Life's Review. Independence: Zion's Printing, (1947).
      pp. 391

An early Mormon history covering the years 1835 to 1896. Unfortunately, Johnson says little of his overland trip in 1848.

Ref.: none

259. [1843] **Johnson, Overton and William H. Winter**   1st: dd,
                                                             rpt.: a
      Route across the Rocky Mountains with a Description of Oregon and California. Lafayette, Ind.: John B. Semans, 1846.
      pp. 152
      rpt.: 1932, Princeton

One of the best of the early overland narratives and one of the two contemporaneously printed accounts of the 1843 migration to Oregon. The first edition is rarely seen for sale, and only a few copies are known to exist.

Ref.: C-p. 315, G-2221, H-J142, WC-122

260. [1849] **(Johnson, Theodore T.)**   1st: b, 3rd: aaa
      Sights in the Gold Region and Scenes by the Way. New York: Baker and Scribner, 1849.
      pp. 278

3rd ed.: includes Oregon material and new title, *California
and Oregon, or Sights in the Gold Region* . . . , 1851,
Philadelphia, pp. 348, f-map (map size, 17 × 14.5
cms.)

The edition of interest here is the third, of which Howes says, "the
3rd, and best, edition contains Thurston's information on the emigrant
trail to Oregon and particulars of the march to Oregon made in 1849,
by the Mounted Rifles." Following the third, there were a number of
other printings.

Ref.: C-p. 315, G-2223-4-5, H-J154, WC-167g

261. [1849] **Johnston, William G.**   1st: cc, rpt.: a
Experiences of a Forty-niner. Pittsburgh, 1892.
pp. 390, 14 plates   50 copies ptd.
rpt.: *Overland to California*, 1948, Oakland, pp. 272

One of the best overland accounts of those journeying to the gold
diggings. Johnston was a member of the first wagon train to enter
California in 1849. Dale Morgan used this diary extensively in his
editing of the Pritchard diary. A blueprint map (to be laid in) was
issued after the book had been distributed and is, in consequence,
lacking in many copies.

Ref.: C-p. 316, G-2229, H-J173, W-113

262. [1856] **Jones, Daniel W.**   aaa
Forty Years Among the Indians. A True yet Thrilling Narrative.
Salt Lake City: Juvenile Instructor Office, 1890.
pp. 400, port. (in some copies)
rpt.: 1960, Los Angeles

Surprised by an early and devastating winter, 145 of the 376 Mormon
Handcart pioneer members of Edward Martin's Company perished. A
dramatic rescue of the survivors took place from a stone refuge near
Devil's Gate, Wyoming. One of these, Daniel Jones, writes firsthand
about this incident, along with many others, as he relates his adventurous life.

Ref.: G-2234, H-J207

263. [1853] **Jones, Rev. Thomas L.**   aa
*From the Gold Mine to the Pulpit. Story of Rev. Thomas L. Jones
. . . Backwoods Methodist Preacher in the Pacific Northwest . . .*
Cincinnati, Ohio: Jennings and Pye, (1904).
pp. 169, frontis, 8 plates, 16 ports.

The Reverend went by ox team from Pike County, Illinois to Oregon
in 1853. He also tells of Idaho's gold mines during the sixties.

Ref.: none

264. [1849]   **Josselyn, Amos Piatt**   a
      *The Overland Journal of Amos Piatt Josselyn. Zanesville, Ohio
      to the Sacramento Valley April 2, 1849 to September 11, 1849.*
      Edited by William J. Barrett II. Baltimore: Gateway Press,
      1978.
      pp. 129, illus.   400 copies
This is in the form of a day-by-day diary. Josselyn speaks of the Stu-
benville and Newark outfits and his journey over Lassen's route. The
Zanesville train was obviously well organized as they suffered no casualties and had a relatively easy time, compared with those who followed the same trail. Also included are his letters from Sacramento
and the mines.
      Ref.: none

265. [1853]   **Judson, Phoebe G.**   1st: c, rpt.: b
      A Pioneer's Search for an Ideal Home. Seattle, 1914.
      pp. 315, frontis
      rpt.: 1925, Bellingham, Wash., pp. 309, frontis
The first eighty or so pages carry a description of Phoebe's travels
across the plains to the Puget Sound area. Only a few copies were
printed for relatives. Both Howes and Graff list only the 1925 edition;
a first edition was, at one time, part of the George W. Soliday collection.
      Ref.: G-2259, H-J274

266. [1847]   **Kane, Thomas L.**   1st: c, 2nd ed.: c-cc
      *The Mormons. A Discourse Delivered Before the Historical Society
      of Pennsylvania March 26, 1850.* (2nd and preferred ed.) Phil-
      adelphia: King & Beard, Printers, 1850.
      pp. 92, wraps
Kane tells of the Mormon migration of 1847 across the plains to Salt
Lake. Although Kane was not a Mormon he joined the Saints on their
journey and preserved an account of the happenings. He was so well
thought of by the Mormon pioneers that they named Kanesville (Council
Bluffs) in his honor. This edition, the second, contains additional
particulars of the trip in an eight page postscript (pp. 85–92). The
first edition has eighty-four pages and was also dated 1850.
      Ref.: G-2263, H-K8, WC-185n

267. [1850] **Keller, George**   1st: dd, rpt.: aa
      *A Trip across the Plains, and Life in California; Embracing a
      Description of the Overland Route; Its Natural Curiosities . . .
      the Gold Mines of California: Its Climate, Soil . . . A Guide of
      the Route from the Missouri River to the Pacific Ocean.* (Mas-
      sillon, Ohio): White's Press, (1851).
      pp. 58, wraps
      rpt.: Biobooks, Oakland, (1955), 500 copies ptd.
J. A. Sullivan states in the foreword of the Biobooks edition that the
last copy of the first edition brought $2600.00 at auction (probably
the W. J. Holiday auction by the Parke-Bernet Galleries, 1954). Sullivan also lists five known copies. Howes indicates he located seven.
Keller tells of Indian attacks; taking Lassen's cutoff; the shortage of
food; and includes some sarcastic references to statements in Ware's
guidebook, a copy of which he appears to have used. He also furnishes
a listing of each member of his party, the "Wayne County Company."
      Ref.: C-p. 323, G-2284, H-K41, WC-199

268. [1849] **Kellogg, George J.**   b
      *Narative (sic) of Geo. J. Kellogg from 1849 to 1915 and Some
      History of Wisconsin since 1835.* (Janesville, Wis.) (1915).
      pp. 38 (including wraps), port., wraps
Kellogg relates his experiences as he hurried overland as a forty-niner,
and his resultant life as a miner in the diggings. Graff says this was
originally printed in the *Janesville Gazette,* and was later reprinted in
a limited edition for friends. Very difficult to locate.
      Ref.: C-p. 859, G-2293, H-K48

269. [1849] **Kelly, William**   cc
      *An Excursion to California over the Prairie, Rocky Mountains
      and Great Sierra Nevada. With a Stroll through the Diggings . . .*
      2 vols. London: Chapman and Hall, 1851.
      pp. 342 and 334, 2 ads.
      2nd ed.: 1852, London, Across the Rocky Mountains, from
            New York to California . . .
      3rd ed.: 1852, London, A Stroll through the Diggings . . .
Volume one contains Kelly's lively recounting of his journey from
Liverpool to New York and overland to California. Vollume two concerns mining and miners. The third ed. begins in California at the
mines.
      Ref.: C-p. 325–26, G-2298, H-K68, P-1026, W-115,
            WC-200

270. [1858] **Kenderdine, T. S.**   bb
        A California Tramp and Later Footprints; or Life on the Plains
        and in the Golden State Thirty Years Ago. Newton, Pa.: pvt.
        ptg., 1888.
        pp. 416, illus. (39 views)
An ox driver with Russell, Majors, and Waddell, Kenderdine went
over the plains to Salt Lake City, supplying the Army during the
Mormon Rebellion. While in Salt Lake, he joined a group of Mormon
freighters and journeyed to California by the southern route. His
narrative is one of the few that tells the unsavory side of life as a
member of one of the great freighting outfits. He saw the members as
"jailbirds, desperados, petty thieves, and a few semirespectable fel-
lows."
        Ref.: C-p. 130, H-K78

271. [1853] **Kennedy, George W.**   aa
        The Pioneer Campfire, in Four Parts: With the Emigrants on the
        Plains. Portland, Oreg.: Marsh Printing, 1913.
        pp. 252, frontis port., 6 plates
These are stories concerning his 1853 overland travels from St. Joseph
to Oregon, and his early days in the area. Kennedy was a member of
the Hubbard-Applegate train.
        Ref.: none

272. [1843] **Kennerly, William Clark**   a
        Persimmon Hill, A Narrative of Old St. Louis and the Far West.
        Edited by Elizabeth Russell. Norman: University of Okla-
        homa, 1948.
        pp. 273, illus.
A preeminent book on the history of the St. Louis area. Kennerly's
uncle was the Clark of Lewis and Clark fame, about whom much is
included. In 1843, when still a teenager, Kennerly became a member
of the overland travels of Sir William Drummond Stewart and adds
many firsthand details respecting the venture. Elizabeth Russell was
the daughter of William and used his writings and diary to construct
this work.
        Ref.: none

273. [1850] **Kilgore, William H.**   aa
        The Kilgore Journey to California in the Year 1850. Edited by
        Joyce Rockwood Muench. New York: Hastings House, 1949.
        pp. 63   1000 copies

Kilgore speaks of the burning of the Mormon "Winterquarters," along with a number of other interesting occurrences he encountered. This was taken from the original manuscript which was in the form of a day-by-day diary. Nicely printed.

Ref.: none

274. [1853] **Kimball, Adelia A.** a
Memoirs of Adelia A. Kimball, One of the Plural Wives of Heber C. Kimball. Edited by Stanley H. B. Kimball. N. p., N. d.
pp. 29

This appears to have been a longer memoir at one time. She mentions her trip of 1853 to the Salt Lake area and tells of subsequent life in Utah. Scarce.

Ref.: none

275. [1845] **King, Anna Marie** a
Covered Wagon Women. Edited by Kenneth L. Holmes. Glendale: Arthur H. Clark Co., 1983.
pp. 272, frontis, f-map, errata slip

This short letter, pages 41–45, is found in Volume I of the ten part series entitled *Covered Wagon Women.* It gives a brief description of the trip overland, and life in Kings Valley of Oregon. She and her husband were members of Meek's misguided train of 1845.

Ref.: none

276. [1846] **King, Stephen and Maria** a
A Letter from Luckiamute Valley in 1846. Portland, N. d.
pp. 5, wraps, printed on rectos only

An item done by the Works Project Administration (WPA) Historical Records Survey of Oregon. The letter was addressed to the Kings' family still residing back in the states, and tells of their six-month overland trip.

Ref.: none

277. [1859] **Kingman, Henry** b
The Travels and Adventures of Henry Kingman, In Search of Colorado and California Gold 1859–1865 . . . Delavan, Morris County, Kans., 1917.
pp. 68, frontis port., 5 plates

Kingman was still a youth of seventeen when he started for Pike's Peak with a company of gold seekers. A number of the party, including the author, changed plans at Independence Rock and continued on to California. An interesting memoir.

Ref.: G-2333, H-K159j

278. [1853] **Kirby, William**   aaa
      Mormonism Exposed and Refuted or True and False Religion
      Contrasted. Forty Years Experience and Observation among the
      Mormons. Nashville, 1893.
      pp. 500
Contains an account of a trip from Kansas City to Salt Lake, possibly
in 1853, and a later return trip east to St. Joseph. A very scarce book.
      Ref.: none

279. [1854] **Kirkpatrick, Thomas Jefferson**   a
      The Kirkpatrick Story; the Day-By-Day Report of the Trek across
      the Plains by the Kirkpatrick Party in 1854. Orland, Calif., 1954.
      pp. 20, double columns, wraps
This is the account of a journey from Springfield, Illinois to St. Joseph,
and from there to Oregon, driving a herd of cattle along the way.
      Ref.: none

280. [1853] **Knight, Mrs. Amelia Stewart**   a
      Women's Diaries of the Westward Journey. Edited by Lillian
      Schlissel. New York: Schocken, (1982).
      pp. 262, frontis, map, illus.
A captivating, but all too brief diary (pages 199 to 216) of a pregnant
woman's journey to Oregon. Already the mother of seven, Mrs. Knight's
entries quite naturally revolve around her family's trials along the trail.
She seems obviously much relieved at journey's end.
      Ref.: none

281. [1852] **(Kuykendall, George B.)**   aa
      History of the Kuykendall Family . . . With Sketches of Colonial
      Times, Old Log Cabin Days, Indian Wars, Pioneer Hardships,
      Social Customs Dress and Mode of Living of the Early Forefathers.
      Portland, Oreg., 1919.
      pp. 645, frontis, ports., illus.
A comprehensive family history that includes the record of an overland
trip.
      Ref.: none

282. [1861] **Lander, Frederick West**   aaa
      Maps and Reports of the Fort Kearney, South Pass, and Honey
      Lake Wagon Road. Letter from the Acting Secretary of the Interior,
      Transmitting Reports and Maps . . . U.S. 36th Congress, 2nd
      Session, House Executive Doc. 64, (Serial 1100), Washing-
      ton: Government Printing Office, 1861.
      pp. 39   250 copies

One of Lander's reports regarding his exploration of the Overland Trail for the best travel route for the not-too-distant railroad.

Ref.: G-2378, H-L58, WC-376:2

283. [1850] **Lane, Samuel A.** aaa
Fifty Years and Over of Akron and Summit County . . . Pioneer Incidents, Interesting Events, Industrial, Commercial, Financial and Educational Process. Akron: Beacon Job Dept., 1892.

pp. 1187, ports., plates

This volume contains a staggering accumulation of local history. Included is the account of Lane's overland journey to Sacramento in 1850 and a list of 350 Akron men who went overland during the years 1849 to 1852.

Ref.: G-2383

284. [1850] **Langsworthy, Franklin** cc
Scenery of the Plains, Mountains and Mines; or a Diary Kept upon the Overland Route to California, by way of the Great Salt Lake . . . in the Years 1850, '51', '52, and '53. Ogdensburgh: J. C. Sprague, 1855.

pp. 324

rpt.: 1932, Princeton

This account is acclaimed by many sources as one of the best written of all overland narratives. The overland description is more than half of the book. The fine Princeton edition usually sells for under $60.00.

Ref.: C-p. 383, G-2392, H-L84, P-1071, W-122, WC-258

285. [1864] **Larimer, Sarah Luse** 1st: bbb, rpt.: aaa
The Capture and Escape; or Life among the Sioux. Philadelphia: Claxton, Remsen & Haffelfinger, 1870.

pp. 252, port., plate

rpt.: 1871, Philadelphia

An exciting narrative. Sarah crossed the plains to Idaho. Her group was massacred at the Little Boxelder, where she was captured by the Indians. She describes her indignities as their captive. When her captors returned her to Ft. Laramie for the reward, open mutiny broke out among the soldiers there upon hearing of her treatment. General Connor ordered three Indian Chiefs shot, then hanged with chains and left that way. This act led to the Indian atrocities of 1866.

Ref.: G-2399, H-L101

286. [1852] **Layton, Christopher**   aa
      *Autobiography of Christopher Layton with an Account of His
      Funeral, a Personal Sketch.* Edited by John Q. Cannon. Salt
      Lake City: Deseret News, 1911.
      pp. 317, port.
A member of the Mormon Battalion, Layton was on the spot to dig
for gold at Sutter's Mill in 1849. Much of the book explores his life
after he reached Salt Lake from St. Louis in 1852.
      Ref.: none

287. [1852] **Leach, A. J.**   aaa
      Early Day Stories. The Overland Trail . . . Norfolk, Neb.: pvt.
      ptg., (1916).
      pp. 244, port., plates
Leach started in Genesee County, Michigan. He tells of joining the
Knapp family as an ox-team driver and of becoming a member of a
party going overland with no rules, regulations, or leader. He tells of
experiences among the Indians; with the dreaded cholera; and with
other events along the trail to Oregon. A good diary.
      Ref.: G-2427, H-L162a

288. [1850] **Lee, L. W.**   aaa
      Autobiography of a Pioneer. Valley View, Tex., 1914.
      pp. 19, wraps
In 1850 Lee went overland for the first time, his journey terminating
at Sacramento. Returning to Missouri in 1852, his next crossing was
in 1857 as captain of the train.
      Ref.: G-2443

289. [1849] **Leeper, David R.**   aaa
      Argonauts of Forty-nine. South Bend, Ind.: J. B. Stoll & Com-
      pany, 1894.
      pp. 145, illus., errata slip
      rpt.: 1950, Columbus, Ohio.
Another forty-niner who choose to take the Lassen cutoff to the
diggings, Leeper set out in a small party of six from South Bend during
the month of February. By the time he reached his destination he was
broke, having spent his last twenty-five cents to ferry across the American River. He describes the people and events of those gold-rush days.
      Ref.: C-p. 388, G-2447, H-L226, P-1116, W-124

290. [1848] **Lempfrit, Honoré-Timothée** a
Honoré-Timothée Lempfrit, O. M. I. His Oregon Trail Journal and Letters from the Pacific Northwest 1848–1853. Edited by Patricia Meyer and Catou Lévesque. Fairfield, Wash.: Ye Galleon Press (1985).
pp. 263, frontis, illus., f-map inside pocket on back cover

Father Lempfrit's diary of his journal covers over 120 pages and is well laced with an abundance of colorful entries. His observations and insights, perhaps because of his profession, are more concerned with the interactions among the people (including Indians) than with the physical aspects of the trail west. Nevertheless, a high interest level is maintained throughout his narrative and the result is a book that is an interesting addition to overland trail literature. Nicely printed.
Ref.: none

291. [1843] **Lenox, Edward H.** bb
Overland to Oregon in the Tracks of Lewis and Clark. A History of the First Emigration to Oregon in 1843. Edited by Robert Whitaker. Oakland: Dowdle Press, 1904.
pp. 69, map, port., illus.
rpt.: (facs.) 1966, Seattle, pp. 80, port., map, plates, wraps, 100 copies ptd.

The author's father, David Thomas Lenox, joined the same train as Marcus Whitman, Jesse Applegate, and others. At the time of this venture Edward was still a small child. The book contains a list of the members of the first emigration party to the Columbia River in 1843.
Ref.: G-2454, H-L255a

292. [1853] **Lewis, Capt. John I.** b
My Garden of Roses, or the Footnotes of Life. N. p., (1907).
pp. 97, illus., wraps

This is the account of a journey from Indiana to California by oxen in 1853. Lewis was the party's wagon master and intersperses his narrative with some detail.
Ref.: none

293. [1846] **Lienhard, Heinrich** a
From St. Louis to Sutter's Fort, 1846. Edited and translated by Edwin G. and Elisabeth K. Gudde. Norman, Okla.: University of Oklahoma Press (1961).
pp. 204, map, illus. (some by William H. Jackson).

Along with the works of Edwin Bryant and J. Q. Thornton, this diary by Lienhard is one of the best records of overland travel during the year 1846. It is the story of five German boys and their varied experiences going overland prior to gold rush. Their small outfit trailed behind the Bryant and Hudspeth pack train and the sixty or so wagons of the Harlan train. Following Lienhard and his friends came the Donners.

Ref.: none

294. [1856] **Linford, James Henry**   aaa
An Autobiography of James Henry Linford, Patriarch, of Kaysville, Utah. N. p., Published by himself, 1919.
pp. 87, port.
rpt.: 1947, Linford Family

Linford tells of being a member of the Willie Handcart Company of 1856 which was stranded in the snow just short of South Pass. His father was one of those who perished. A monument now marks the site along the trail east of Atlantic City, Wyoming.

Ref.: none

295. [1849] **Little, James A.**   b
From Kirtland to Salt Lake City . . . Salt Lake City: Juvenile Instructor Office, 1890.
pp. 260, illus.

Interesting and enlightening overland narrative to Salt Lake City. Little converted to Mormonism in the early part of 1849. He then traveled from St. Louis to Kanesville, and from there to the Salt Lake area, arriving in October of the same year.

Ref.: G-2510, H-L382

296. [1851] **Lobenstine, William C.**   ccc
Extracts from the Diary of William C. Lobenstine December 31, 1851–58. Biographical sketch by Belle W. Lobenstine. N. p.: pvt. ptg. (1920).
pp. 101, port., illus.

Lobenstine traveled overland by way of the Platte River and Fort Bridger. Reaching California, he tells of mining life during the years 1852–54.

Ref.: C-p. 394, G-2516, H-L410

297. [1847] **(Lockley, Fred)**   a
To Oregon by Ox Team in '47; the Story of the Coming of the Hunt Family to the Oregon Country and the Experiences of G. W. Hunt in the Gold Diggings of California in 1849. Portland: pvt. ptg., N. d.
pp. 16, wraps

G. W. Hunt was a relative of the well known Wilson Price Hunt, early explorer of the West. This short recollection speaks briefly of the trip overland, and later trips to the diggings near Shasta.

Ref.: none

298. [1864] **Lomas, Thomas J.** cc
Recollections of a Busy Life . . . (Cresco, Iowa, 1923).
pp. 220, ports.
The author relates memories of his 1864 wagon trip to Honey Lake, California. It seems that only a small number of copies were printed for his relations, making the book very scarce today.

Ref.: G-2523, H-L436

299. [1849] **(Long, Margaret)** a
The Shadow of the Arrow. Caldwell: Caxton, 1941.
pp. 310, illus.
2nd ed.: 1950, Caldwell, pp. 354, illus.
Contains most of the diary of forty-niner Sheldon Young (pages 241–63). Young started from Joliet, went through Salt Lake City, and describes his route from there to Death Valley. The second edition may be preferred as it also includes as Appendix C the brief Nusbaumer diary, and a discussion of the Bigler "journal."

Ref.: E-p. 106

300. [1852] **Long, Mary Jane** aaa
Crossing the Plains in the Year of 1852 with Ox Teams. Mc-Minnville, Oreg., (1915). (date uncertain)
pp. 17, port., wraps
At the head of the title: "A True Story." A scarce pamphlet. Though a copy was not available for verification, the reported height of this book is 17½ cms.

Ref.: none

301. [1853] **Longsworth, Basil N.** aa
Diary of Basil Nelson Longsworth March 15, 1853 to January 22, 1854 Covering the Period of His Migration from Ohio to Oregon. Denver: D. E. Harrington, 1927.
pp. 43, wraps
Graff says, "This is a detailed day-by-day contemporary diary—a real overland." Contains details of the country, trails, deaths, murders, drownings, and more. In 1938 this was reissued (although called the "First Publication") by the Historical Records Survey of the Works Project Administration (WPA) with Longsworth's name printed as Longworth. (Portland, pp. 68, wraps)

Ref.: G-2530, H-L458

302.   [1850] **Loomis, Leander W.**   aa
        A *Journal of the Birmingham Emigrating Company*. Edited by
        Edgar M. Ledyard. Salt Lake City: (Legal Printing), 1928.
        pp. 198, frontis port., 16 plates, large f-map, 1000 copies
        ptd.
A record of an overland journey made in 1850 from Birmingham,
Iowa to Sacramento. The map shows the route followed, and the
plates include photographs of the party members, sights along the
trail, and graves of some who died along the way. The party took both
the Sublette and Hudspeth short cuts. William Clayton's emigrant
guide for the Latter Day Saints is included as an appendix. The first
300 copies carry a signed and numbered bookplate bearing the Loomis
Crest and signatures of the daughter of the journalist and the daughter
of the first Captain.
        Ref.: C-p. 396, H-L464, P-1167, W-128

303.   [1853] **Looney, Mrs. M. A.**   aaa
        A *Trip Across the Plains in 1853* . . . Albany, Oreg.: Albany
        Printing, 1912.
        pp. (7)
A copy of this book to verify the collation could not be found.
        Ref.: none

304.   [1850] **Lord, Elizabeth**   bbb
        Reminiscences of Eastern Oregon. Portland: Irwin-Hodson, 1903.
        pp. 155, 14 plates (including frontis)
Only a few copies of this book were printed for the author. She tells
in detail of her overland trip by oxen with the Laughlin party along
the trail to Oregon. Also included are extracts from the diary of W.
C. Laughlin, 1856–62, and family records for the Laughlin, Yeargain,
Woodford, Bucker, and Madison families, plus some stories of later
life and adventures in the territory.
        Ref.: G-2534, H-L468

305.   [1849] **Lorton, William B.**   aa
        Over the Salt Lake Trail in the Fall of '49. Los Angeles, 1957.
        pp. 18, illus.   150 copies
This is a letter describing Lorton's hardships on the trail. The book
was printed as a keepsake for members of the Zamorano Club, and is
part of the "Scraps of California" series.
        Ref.: E-p. 107

306. [1853] **Love, Helen M. (Stewart)**   a
      Diary of Helen Stewart, 1853. Eugene, Oreg.: Lane County
      Historical Society, N. d.
      pp. 26, mounted facs.
Helen was sister to Agnes and Elizabeth Stewart who also went overland in 1853 and wrote about it (*see* 445). Reportedly, this account
was only recently discovered.
      Ref.: none

307. [1850] **Loveland, Cyrus C.**   aa
      *California Trail Herd; The 1850 Missouri to California Journal
      of Cyrus C. Loveland.* Edited by Richard C. Dillon. Los Gatos:
      Talisman Press, 1961.
      pp. 137, illus., e-map   750 copies
The account of a cattle drive from Missouri to California, undoubtedly
one of the first.
      Ref.: none

308. [1864] **Luster, Mary R.**   aaa
      *The Autobiography of Mary R. Luster, Written in her Eighty-first
      and Eighty-second Years.* Springfield, 1935.
      pp. 197, frontis
Mary traveled overland from Missouri to Idaho, staying there only
four years before returning.
      Ref.: none

309. [1853] **Lyman, Esther**   a
      Esther Brakeman Lyman Diary/Joseph Lyman Letter/Genealogies.
      Eugene, Oreg.: Lane County Historical Society, 1960.
      pp. 27 (variously numbered), ports., ptd. on rectos only
      rpt.: 1966, same
Information is given here concerning the Lyman and Wadsworth fam-
ily trees. Esther's diary adds many details to the episode of the 1853
"Lost Wagon Train." Hers is the story of a member of one of the latter
wagons of those struggling through the unbroken mountain trails in
Oregon. She tells briefly of the rampant hunger and the relief brought
by the rescue parties. This diary, as with the other Lane County
Historical Society Publications, is in typescript.
      Ref.: none

310. [1860] **Lyman, Vincent P.**   bbb
     Diary of Vincent P. Lyman in 1860 As He Went on the Overland
     Emigrant Wagon Train from Kansas to California. N. p., N. d.
     pp. 34, bound in limp suede
His original destination was Pike's Peak, but en route that was changed
to California. His party reached Marysville the first week in September
after a somewhat uneventful journey. This is another one of those
obscure overland books not found listed in any of the major bibliog-
raphies.
     Ref.: none

311. [1849] **McCall, A. J.**   b
     The Great California Trail in 1849. Wayside Notes of an Ar-
     gonaut. Bath, N.Y., 1882.
     pp. 86, wraps
A description of his trip westward to look for gold. McCall started at
St. Joseph and traveled via South Pass, Salt Lake, and the Humboldt.
This is the same A. J. McCall who wrote *Pick and Pan. Trip to the*
Diggings in 1849 . . . , a sequel that begins at Sutter's Fort.
     Ref.: C-p. 402

312. [1852] **McClung, Zarah**   ddd
     Travels Across the Plains in 1852. St. Louis: Chambers and
     Knapp, 1854.
     pp. 34 (including front wrap)
The Wagner-Camp-Becker bibliography reports the only known copy
is in the Kentucky University Library. Therefore, the value stated
above is arbitrary. McClung traveled to Russell's diggings, near Vol-
cano, in California.
     Ref.: C-p. 872, H-M48, WG-240b

313. [1853] **McClure, Andrew S.**   a
     Diary of Andrew S. McClure, 1829–1898. Eugene, Oreg.: Lane
     County Historical Society, 1959.
     pp. 142, ports., wraps, ptd. on rectos only
     rpt.: 1973, same
Even though unfinished, Andrew McClure's diary is one of the most
complete and detailed accounts published of the overland trek to
Oregon. His party, guided by Elijah Elliot, followed the tracks of the
1845 Meeks train over the Meeks cutoff. This party too became lost
and suffered immensely. Accordingly, this large party of emigrants has
become known as "The Lost Wagon Train" (of 1853) or "Elliot's Lost
Wagon Train." McClure details the wanderings of a small group, sent
ahead for supplies, struggling through the waterless desert and over

brushbound mountains. (See also the journal of Benjamin Owen, who suffered alongside McClure.) In 1978 another section of McClure's diary was found and inserted as a 50 page addition. It covers the early days of the trip, the 21st of March to the 7th of May. This current insertion appears to have replaced the diary of James McClure which was included as part of the first printing. The Andrew McClure diary is an important record, and engaging overland reading.

Ref.: none

314. [1862] **McComas, E. S.**   aa
Journal of Travel. Portland: Champoeg Press, 1954.
pp. 83, frontis, illus.   500 copies
McComas traveled to Oregon to escape from involvement in the Civil War. He tells of the trip, which, considering the alternative, he was prepared to enjoy. The illustrations, from the author's sketches, are apparently the only known contemporary pictorial record of life in the Powder River Mines. Nicely printed by Lawton Kennedy.

Ref.: none

315. [1849] **McCoy, Samuel**   bb
Pioneering on the Plains . . . the Overland Trip to California.
(Kaukauna, Wis., 1924).
pp. 60, port., wraps
McCoy began his travels at Independence. This book also contains the letters of John A. Johnson, who describes his journey and later life in California. (These two entries are unrelated.) It also contains the letters of brothers John, Alexander, and William McCoy relating their adventures while traveling to Santa Fe, Mexico, and the west coast.

Ref.: C-p. 872, H-M66

316. [1849] **(McDonald, Frank V.)**   c
Notes Preparatory to a Biography of Richard Hayes McDonald of San Francisco, California. Vol. I. Cambridge: Ptd. for private distribution, 1881.
pp. 119, 34 plates   150 copies
A rare and important addition to the overland story. McDonald was a member of the Turner and Allen overland party, but left it at Ft. Laramie, and with two others (C. H. Swift and Louis Sloss) continued over the trail to California, reaching it on July 18, 1849. He speaks of trying to help the Nauvoo Mormons in 1846, and also has something on the Donner tragedy. Volume two never appeared.

Ref.: C-p. 406, G-2598, H-M82

317.   [1850]   **McGee, Joseph Hedger**   aaa
       Story of the Grand River Country 1821–1905. Memoirs of Joseph Hedger McGee. (Gallintin, Mo., 1909).
       pp. 63, port., wraps
McGee's memoirs include the recounting of his trip overland in 1850.
       Ref.: G-2608, H-M101

318.   [1846]   **(McGlashan, Charles F.)**   1st: cc, 2nd ed.: bbb
       History of the Donner Party. Truckee, Calif.: Crowley and McGlashan, (1879).
       pp. 193, map, illus.
       2nd ed.: 1880, San Francisco, plates added.
This has been included here not only because it is one of the most highly regarded books concerning an epic event of Western history, but also since it is, in part, based on actual interviews and correspondence with the survivors. McGlashan was editor of the Truckee *Republican.*
       Ref.: G-2610, H-M102, P-53, Z-53

319.   [1849]   **McIlhany, Edward**   b
       Recollections of a '49er. Kansas City, Mo.: Hailman Printing Co., 1908.
       pp. 212, frontis, plates
McIlhany, "one of the last old boys," as he calls himself, was a member of the Charleston Company, the same outfit that Vincent Geiger and Wakeman Bryarly belonged to. His memories regarding that trip occupy the first forty or so pages of this book.
       Ref.: C-p. 407, G-2614, H-M111, W-133

320.   [1850]   **McKeeby, Lemuel Clarke**   aa
       The Memoirs of Lemuel Clarke McKeeby. San Francisco: California Historical Society, 1924.
       pp. 75, wraps, f-map
McKeeby traveled from Milwaukee to California during 1850. This is one of the earliest works published separately by the California Historical Society.
       Ref.: C-p. 873

321.   [1850]   **McKinstry, Byron N.**   a
       The California Gold Rush Overland Diary of Byron McKinstry, 1850–52, with a Biographical Sketch and Comment on a Modern Tracing of His Overland Travel, by His Grandson Bruce L. McKinstry; With a Foreword by Ray Allen Billington. Glendale: Arthur H. Clark Co., 1975.
       pp. 401, frontis port., many plates

Byron McKinstry left Illinois in March of 1850 on a trek to Hangtown. This well done book is engrossing on two counts. One is the inclusion of the original McKinstry diary; and the other is Bruce's tracing of his grandfather's journey. His comments and findings, regarding the trail, follow, in sequence, the daily notations by the elder McKinstry. It makes for great reading as it, in effect, spans over 100 years.

Ref.: P-1210

322.   [1846]   **McKinstry, George**   bbb
Thrilling and Tragic Journal . . . Written on a Journey Overland to California in 1846–47 . . . West Hoboken: A. Bieber, (1917). pp. 1, triple columns, one side, rose colored.
65 copies (63 on rose paper; 1 on yellow, 1 on gold)

This is the diary of Patrick Breen, member of the Donner party. McKinstry, who had traveled overland in 1846, was sheriff of the Sacramento District of California in 1847. Breen gave his diary to McKinstry on arriving at Sutter's Fort in 1847, and when it was later printed in a St. Louis newspaper it carried McKinstry's name. Another name, John Sinclair, is also sometimes erroneously given credit for writing the short Breen diary. "The Diary of George McKinstry with a letter to P. B. Reading" is part of Dale L. Morgan's *Overland in 1846: Diaries and Letters of the California Trail,* 1963, Georgetown, 2 vols. (see pages 199–218). This is the actual diary of George McKinstry, and is quite abbreviated, beginning on May 12th and ending abruptly on June 30, 1846. He was traveling in the same party as J. Quinn Thornton.

Ref.: C-p. 408, P-1211

323.   [1862]   **McLaughlin, Daniel**   aa
Sketch of a Trip from Omaha to Salmon River. Chicago: Gordon Martin, 1954.
pp. 18   150 copies

This account was printed for private distribution by Graff and includes notes by him. McLaughlin tells of Indians and of his experiences seeking gold.

Ref.: none

324.   [1849]   **McWilliams, John**   b-bb
Recollections . . . Experiences in California . . . Princeton: Princeton University Press, (1919).
pp. 186, port.

McWilliams went overland to Oregon in 1849, and from there joined the rush to the California gold mines. Much of the book relates his experiences in these early mining camps, as well as an earlier look at pioneer life in Tazewell County, Illinois (near Peoria) where Mc-Williams was raised. A scarce book.

Ref.: C-p. 410, G-2651, H-M194

325. [1849] **Manly, William L.**   b
      Death Valley in 49. San Jose: Pacific Tree and Vine Co., 1894.
      pp. 498, port., and three illus.

One of the great books of Western Americana. Important as a firsthand observation of a famous overland party and its famous (mis)adventures. Also important as a desert book, since this party is given credit for naming Death Valley, and as an early book of travel and adventure.

Ref.: C-p. 412, E-p. 110–11, G-2670, H-M255, P-1226,
      W-136

326. [1859] **Marcy, Randolph B.**   1st: c, Eng. ed.: bbb, 3rd: bb
      The Prairie Traveler. A Handbook for Overland Expeditions. With
      Maps, Illustrations, and Itineraries of the Principal Routes between
      the Mississippi and the Pacific. New York: Harper & Bros., 1859.
      pp. 340, plates, f-map (size, 22.5 × 37 cms.)
      Eng. ed.: 1860, London, pp. 230 & 2 (ads.)
      3rd ed.: 1861, New York, pp. 381, f-map

Marcy's book well illustrates how the massive Western movement had created a demand for alternate and/or more direct routes. He lists here twenty-eight routes of travel, a far cry from the two or three advisable roads of the 1840s.

Ref.: G-2676, H-M279, WC-335

327. [1859] **Mathews, Edward J.**   cc
      Crossing the Plains . . . in '59. N. p., pvt. ptg., (1930) (date
      uncertain).
      pp. 91   50 copies ptd. (number uncertain)

A relatively recent, but scarce, account. Mathews left Iowa with a group originally headed for Pike's Peak. Discouraged by reports heard along the way, they changed their destination to the West Coast. Mathews spent some time in Virginia City where he was successful until, fed up with Indian troubles, he moved to the Esmeralda area.

Ref.: G-2711, H-M415

328. [1849] **Matthews, Leonard**   1st ed.: b, 2nd: aa
      A Long Life in Review. (St. Louis: pvt. ptg., 1927).
      pp. 178, photos, frontis.
      2nd ed.: 1928

There is no date or place of printing listed; however, the introduction indicates St. Louis, and the frontis is dated December 17, 1927. Matthews speaks of the Mormons at Nauvoo, the trip overland to California, and experiences in the diggings.

Ref.: G-2720

329. [1857] **Maxwell, William A.** aa
Crossing the Plains. Days of '57. San Francisco: Sunset Publishing, (1915).
pp. 179, illus., wraps (brown)

This contains much colorful description. Particularly outstanding is Maxwell's narration of an incident involving justice on the trail. No stalling is encountered here, no conniving lawyers present, and punishment soon follows the emigrant verdict. Maxwell spends a couple of chapters telling this story of crime and punishment, and his record of such an event, if not unique in itself among overland journals, is singular for the dramatic way he unfolds it.

Ref.: C-p. 240, G-2728, H-680 (1954), P-1254

330. [1852] **Meeker, Ezra** 1906 ptg.: bb, 1907 ptg.: aa
The Ox Team or the Old Oregon Trail 1852–1906. Omaha, (1906).
pp. 248, port., illus.

The first printing was in October, 1906; the second, third, and fourth printings all followed in 1907. The book was later reprinted with title variations.

This is an account of the author's trip across the plains at the age of twenty-two, and of the retracing of the trail in 1906 with an ox team at the age of seventy-six. The text is somewhat disjointed. However, the book is still interesting due to the heroic nature of the venture.

Ref.: none

331. [1849] **Merkley, Christopher** aaa
Biography of Christopher Merkley, Written by Himself. Salt Lake City, 1887.
pp. 46, wraps

Merkley describes the Mormon problems in Missouri and that group's subsequent movements until forced to look further west. He tells of his trip over the plains in 1849 and of later travels among the Indians.

Ref.: G-2755, H-M537

332. [1849] **Meyer, George**   cc
      Autobiography of George Meyer, across the Plains with an Ox
      Team in 1849. His Success in the Gold Fields of California.
      Shenandoah, Iowa: The Open Door, 1908.
      pp. 29, 2 ports., wraps
Meyer, a member of a small group, writes a brief diary of his trip. At
the end of the journey he spent only about one year at the Coloma
mines.
Some asking prices far exceed that above and are most likely based
on the rarity, versus the importance of this item. It is not clear how
many copies are available, but it would appear, after somewhat diligent
searching, there are only a few.
                Ref.: C-p. 875, G-2777, H-M573

333. [1848] **Miller, Jacob**   a
      Journal of Jacob Miller. Edited by Joseph R. and Elna Miller.
      N. p., 1967.
      pp. 199
Miller wrote these reminiscences in 1909. He speaks of living in
Nauvoo and of traveling to Utah in 1848.
                Ref.: none

334. [1849] **(Mitchell, Samuel A., Pub.)**   ccc
      Description of Oregon and California, Embracing an Account of
      the Gold Regions. Philadelphia: Cowperthwait & Co., 1849.
      pp. 76, f-map (53 × 49.2 cms.)
The map shows the emigrant route from Missouri to California and
depicts California as what is today Nevada, Utah, Arizona, and a little
of New Mexico.
                Ref.: G-2839, H-M687

335. [1850] **Moorman, Madison Berryman**   aa
      Journal of Madison Berryman Moorman 1850–1851. Edited by
      Irene D. Paden. San Francisco: California Historical Society,
      1948.
      pp. 150, f-map
The importance of this diary lies in the fact that Moorman was one
of the few who decided to try the Hastings cutoff through the long
desert stretches of western Utah, and then kept a journal while doing
so. A nicely printed book.
                Ref.: P-1326, W-146

336. [1846] **(Morgan, Dale L., Ed.)**   aaa
      Overland in 1846: Diaries and Letters of the California Trail. 2
      vols. Georgetown: Talisman Press, 1963.
      pp. 825, 4 maps in pocket, f-map, illus., 1000 sets ptd.

An important overland work of the first magnitude. Contains an
abundance of information on the emigrants of 1846 never before
published in book form. Volume one includes the J. M. Shiveley
Guidebook (pp. 734–742) and the diaries of:

    1. Patrick Breen, pp. 306–22.
    2. Nicholas Carringer, pp. 143–58.
    3. John Craig, pp. 133–42.
    4. Thomas Holt, pp. 189–98.
    5. John R. McBride, pp. 90–100.
    6. George McKinstry, pp. 199–218.
    7. James Mathers, pp. 219–36.
    8. Hiram O. Miller/James Frazier Reed, pp. 245–77 and
       289–305 (Reed only).
    9. Virgil Pringle, pp. 159–88.
  10. Virginia Reed, pp. 278–88.
  11. William E. Taylor, pp. 118–37.

Volume two consists mostly of letters. The four reproduced maps in
the pocket (two sheets, printed on both sides) are the rare T. H.
Jefferson map.
There was also a special edition of 100 copies done in morocco with
marbled boards that sells in the $200.00–$300.00 range.
    Ref.: P-1333

337. [1849] **Morgan, Mrs. Martha M., Ed.**   ddd
      A Trip across the Plains . . . San Francisco: Pioneer Press,
      1864.
      pp. 31, ptd. wraps

The original journal was kept by the author's husband, Jesse. It is a
short, but honest account of their trip. For example: "Here Captain
Geo. Hancock got the big head, went on, and left all the company
behind." They left St. Joseph late in May and wintered in Salt Lake
City. In April of 1850 they left Salt Lake for the Humboldt (called
St. Mary's in the Journal), and followed that route to California. Also
included is a short diary of a trip to California by way of Panama in
1854 and a selection of religious songs. Her husband has been identified
as the author of the diary in *The Polygamist's Victim* (1872, San Francisco) in which the same trip is recounted. See also chap. XIV of
Manly's *Death Valley in 49* in which M. S. McMahon speaks of traveling
with the Morgans to California. Book size is 21.5 × 13.5 cm., and
only five or six copies are known to exist.
    Ref.: H-M805, WC-402

338. [1864]   **(Morrill, Rosa Neil)**   bb
     Mary Jane, Pioneer. (Venice, Calif.) Neil Book, (1942).
     pp. 382, frontis of Mary Jane Welty, photos
It appears only an armful of this book was printed. It is typescript.
The photo descriptions are handwritten, and the second title page is
hand-colored (the picture is reproduced in black outline on the cover).
This is an embroidered telling of the true overland journey of Mary
Jane and John Welty, containing an abundance of dialogue. The author
apparently had a close relationship with Mary Jane, who passed away
in 1937 at the age of ninety-six, as there are related many details of
family history. The Welty family, caught in October snowstorms, were
persuaded to winter at Alder Gulch, Montana. Deciding that "any
other place in the world must be better," they struggled to Salt Lake
and from there by the southern route to California arriving in 1865.
A unique portrait of a pioneer woman, and a very, very scarce book.
     Ref.: none

339. [1853]   **Mossman, Isaac**   aa
     A Pony Expressman's Recollections. Portland: Lawton Kennedy,
     1955.
     pp. 55, f-map, illus.   500 copies
Mossman traveled in a group called the Miller party. Their destination
was Oregon. For some time he was owner of an express company.
     Ref.: none

340. [1846]   **Murphy, Virginia Reed**   aa
     Across the Plains in the Donner Party. Palo Alto: Lewis Os-
     bourne, N. d.
     pp. 56, illus.   1400 copies ptd.
Some forty-five years following the Donner tragedy Virginia Murphy
wrote these plaintive recollections for *Century Magazine.* Her father
was James Reed, an important figure in the event. Attractively printed
with a foreword by George Stewart.
     Ref.: P-1352

341. [1852]   **(Myres, Sandra L., Ed.)**   a
     Ho for California. San Marino: Huntington Library, 1980.
     pp. 314, illus., e-maps
This book is composed of women's overland diaries from the Huntington Library's wealth of original manuscripts. Pages 49 to 93 contain
the 1852 journal of Mary Stuart Bailey. An interesting narrative by
one who apparently would have much rather forgone the experience.
     Ref.: none

342. [1857] **(Myres, Sandra L., Ed.)** a
Ho for California. San Marino: Huntington Library, 1980.
pp. 314, illus., e-maps
Pages 93 to 188 contain the diary of Helen Carpenter, titled, "A Trip across the Plains in an Ox-wagon in 1857." This is a delightful journal by a young woman full of grit and spirit. Indeed, her optimistic outlook makes it difficult for the reader not to urge her vicariously onward as she travels over South Pass, along the Humboldt, and into California by way of the Truckee. Nicely printed.
Ref.: none

343. [1852] **Nelson, James Horace, Jr.** a
Autobiography of James Horace Nelson, Senior, Son of David Nelson and Mary Thompson Miller Nelson, Born at Jacksonville, Morgan County, Illinois, U.S.A., March 28, 1893. (N. p., 1944).
pp. 139 (?)
Generally concerned with Nelson's life as a Mormon, this account adds little to the overland experience. It was written at the close of the last century with pages 123 to 139 as an appendix relating the facts of his death.
Ref.: none

344. [1850] **Newton, John Marshall** bb
Memoirs of John Marshall Newton. Copyright 1913 by John M. Stevenson. (Cambridge, N.Y.), 1913.
pp. 91, ports., 7 plates
The memoirs include Newton's 1850 overland trip from Ohio to California, and his life there for the next two years. Pages 89 to 91 contain a completion of the memoirs by Ellen Huldah Newton.
Ref.: C-p. 454, G-3020, H-N130

345. [1860] **Nibley, Charles Wilson** aa
Reminiscences. Charles W. Nibley 1849–1931. Salt Lake City, 1934.
pp. 198
Even though his parents had joined the Mormon faith in 1844, Nibley, who became a notable Mormon, tells of attending the Baptist church before journeying to Utah in 1860.
Ref.: none

346. [1854] **Nobles, William H.**   dd
     Speech of the Hon. Wm. H. Nobles, together with Other Doc-
     uments, Relative to an Emigrant Route to California and Oregon,
     Through Minnesota Territory. Printed by Order of the Council.
     St. Paul: Olmstead & Brown, 1854.
     pp. 13, wraps (yellow)
According to Thomas W. Streeter, noted collector of Americana,
Nobles had discovered a new route over the Sierras that began about
eighty miles above the Humboldt Sink, and therefore missed much
of the desert. This pamphlet tells about it, saying it was first used by
emigrants in 1852.
     Ref.: G-3024, WC-241

347. [1852] **Norton, Lewis A.**   aaa
     Life and Adventures of Col. L. A. Norton. Oakland: Pacific
     Press, 1887.
     pp. 492, frontis port.
Chapters 27 to 29 include a brief synopsis of his overland trip to
Hangtown (Placerville) as the captain of the Rough and Ready Company. Norton's egotistical heralding of many of the events of the
journey, as well as those of the rest of his life, make for hard swallowing.
This was reprinted as "My Overland Trip to the Gold Fields of California in 1852," in the *Pony Express Courier*, Placerville, Calif., Vol.
1, No. 4–5.
     Ref.: C-p. 457, G-3042, H-N210

348. [1854] **Nott, Manfred Allen**   1st: c, 2nd ed.: b
     Across the Plains in '54. N. p., N. d.
     pp. 76, pictorial wraps
     2nd ed.: San Francisco, N. d., pp. 232, port.
A very rare overland. Both Howes and Graff list only the second
edition, Howes states that the second edition is "apparently the first
in book form." The first edition can be determined by the lines found
on page 76: "I shall tell you how we suffered, bled and almost died
for the cause in my next story, which I shall call: The Captive
Maidens. . . ." "The Captive Maidens" occupies pages 135–232 in the
greatly expanded second edition. Howes mentions that almost all
copies were destroyed in the San Francisco fire of 1906. This may also
be true of the first edition. Nott's story is subtitled, "A Story for Young
People of Early Emigration to California," and includes, among others,
adventures with Indians and bears. Nott was a member of the Hendrix
train and tells of being guided, and befriended, by Jim Bridger.
     Ref.: C-p. 457, G-3045, H-N213

349. [1849] **Nusbaumer, Louis**   aa
      Valley of Salt, Memories of Wines: A Journal of Death Valley,
      1849. Edited by George Koenig. Berkeley: Friends of the
      Bancroft Library, 1967.
      pp. 67, frontis, f-map, 3 plates (photos by Ansel Adams)
Nusbaumer's diary provides the only firsthand account of the party
that not only lost its way, but some of whose members lost their lives
on the way to the west coast. He was with William Manly and the
forty-niners who attempted the shortcut through the unknown desert
area—which was to become known as Death Valley. The sketchy
format of this diary has prevented it from becoming more widely
recognized.
      Ref.: E-p. 122, P-1480

350. [1862] **Nye-Starr, Kate**   d
      A Self Sustaining Woman; or the Experience of Seventy-two Years
      . . . Chicago: Illinois Printing and Binding Co., 1888.
      pp. 161, port.
Paher, in his bibliography on Nevada, states that only two copies of
this book are known. Kate and her family, from Niagara, N.Y., traveled
to Salt Lake where she speaks of meeting such well known Mormons
as Brigham Young and the infamous Porter Rockwell. When she reached
Carson City she stayed in the same rooming house as Sam Clemens.
She was the sister of Nevada's Governor Nye.
      Ref.: G-3056, H-N232, P-1481

351. [1854] **Oaks, George Washington**   a
      Man of the West. Reminiscences of George Washington Oaks.
      Edited by Arthur Woodward, (Tucson: Arizona Pioneers, 1956).
      pp. 65, frontis port.
Oaks traveled to Marysville, California as a boy of fourteen. He apparently remembered little of the trip, as he gives it only a slight
mention.
      Ref.: none

352. [1853] **Owen, Benjamin Franklin**   a
      My Trip across the Plains March–October 1853. Eugene, Oreg.:
      Lane County Pioneer Society, N. d.
      pp. 60, port., heavy wraps, typescript
      rpt.: 1967, same
Owen was a member of the "Lost Wagon Train" and, with seven others,
suffered many hardships and deprivations in his attempt to reach Oregon after leaving the main party. One of the most detailed and
interesting diaries in its description of the sufferings that could be
encountered by one on the trail.
      Ref.: none

353. [1843] **Owens-Adair, Mrs. Bethenia A.** aa
Some of Her Experiences. (Portland): Mann and Beach, (1906).
pp. 537, 7 ports.
Mrs. Owens-Adair, who later became a doctor and wrote extensively
on sterilization, tells what she remembers about her overland trip.
Ref.: none

354. [1849] **Packard, Major W. and G. Larison** cc
Early Emigration to California 1849–50. Bloomington, Ill.,
1928.
pp. 23, 3 ports., wraps (tan)   30 copies
A pamphlet that is rarely seen for sale. It is the personal narrative of
an overland trip to Hangtown along with some later experiences in
the life of Major Packard. The biography of G. (Greenberry) Larison
contains a short account of his overland highlights of 1850. Packard's
"Early Emigration to California" was originally published in 1899 in
War Record of McLean County, and Other Papers, while Larison's biography was first contained in Prof. Duis's "The Good Old Times in
McLean County." (Information taken from Prefatory Note by Milo
Custer.)
Ref.: C-p. 880, G-3157, H-P6

355. [1849] **(Page, Elizabeth)** a
Wagons West. New York: Farrar & Rinehart, (1930).
pp. 361, photos
This contains the unedited narrative of Henry Page's journey to California, from letters written home to his wife. Page was a member of
the "Green and Jersey County Company." The book also includes brief
entries from E. I. (or E. L.), who was E. I. Bowman, a member of
the same company; Joseph Hackney, Charles A. Kirkpatrick, and
Henry Tappan.
Ref.: P-1504, W-151

356. [1852] **Palmer, Harriet Scott** bb
Crossing the Great Plains by Ox Wagon. (Seattle): I. R. Archer,
(1931).
pp. 9, wraps
The last time it was offered for sale (and possibly the last one sold)
was in a 1953 Eberstadt Catalog. The price was $75.00.
Ref.: none

357. [1845] **Palmer, Joel**   1st: dd, 2nd ed.: d
Journal of Travels over the Rocky Mountains to the Mouth of the Columbia River, Made during the Years 1845 and 1846. Cincinnati: J. A. and U. P. James, Walnut Street, Between Fourth and Fifth, 1847.

pp. 189, wraps, errata slip
rpt.: 1906, Cleveland, pp. 311, Vol. XXX of Thwaite's Early Western Travel series.

An important guidebook for over a decade, this was also considered the best narrative by those who headed for Oregon in 1845. Palmer's party was one of the first over the Barlow Road in Oregon.

The first edition, first printing, has 1847 on the paper cover not overprinted or changed, and the errata slip, although Wagner-Camp-Becker hints that the errata slip may not have been in the first copies taken in haste by Palmer from the printers. Errata information can be found in Graff, page 478.

Ref.: G-3171, H-P47, WC-136.

358. [1853] **Parker, Basil G.**   cc
Life and Adventures of Basil G. Parker, an Autobiography. Plano, Calif.: F. W. Reed, 1902.

pp. 88, port., wraps

Includes the accounts of his two overland journeys, the first in 1853, another in 1857, along with stories of pioneer life in California. The author wrote this at the age of seventy-seven. It was privately printed and is quite rare. The copy from the collection of W. J. Holliday sold in 1954 for $225.00.

Ref.: none

359. [1846] **Parkman, Francis**   1st: ddd, best rpt.: c
The California and Oregon Trail. New York: George P. Putnam's, 1849.

pp. 488, wraps (2 parts) cloth (1 part), 6 ad. pages, pp. 1 and 2 in front, 3–6 at end of book, frontis.

anr. ed: 1849, New York and London (on title page).

anr. ed.: 1849, 10 ad. pages (pp. 3–10) also issued with no ads., no frontis, no English title.

2nd ptg.: 1849, no ads. in front, 7 ads. at end, numbered 1–8 (error for 7), pp. 436 and 437 have bad type, 500 copies.

3rd ptg.: 1849, no printer's imprint on verso of title page and "see p. 290" on frontis.

3rd ed.: 1852, Boston, pp. 448.
4th ed.: 1872, Boston, pp. 371.
Best rpt.: 1892, Boston, *The Oregon Trail,* 9 plates, pp. 411,
 illus. by Frederick Remington.

A classic book on the west, and one of the most important concerning overland travel. Parkman graphically tells of wagon trains, Indians, trappers, and other features of the west as he experienced them. He speaks often, and highly, of the guide, Henry Chatillon. Bernard DeVoto called it "One of the exuberant masterpieces of American literature."

 Ref.: G-3201, H-P97, WC-170:1a

360. [1850] **Peacock, William**   a
 *The Peacock Letters April 7, 1850 to Jan. 4, 1852; Fourteen
 Letters Written . . . to His Wife Susan . . .* Stockton: San Joaquin Pioneer and Historical Society, 1950.
 pp. 32, ports. (mounted), wraps (grey)

Much is to be said in favor of letters recording one's trip to the mines versus the diary consisting of directions for those still at home who may follow. The latter form quite often results in a cold, factual reporting of the day's events; the former, as in these Peacock letters, because they were intended as personal communications, lean heavily on thoughts, feelings, and private observations. Accordingly, we find ourselves sharing Peacock's disillusionment with the rigors of the jour-ney, and overall opportunities at the mines.

 Ref.: none

361. [1849] **Pearson, Gustavas C.**   aa
 *Overland in 1849; from Missouri to California by the Platte River
 and the Salt Lake Trail, an Account from the Letters of Gustavas
 C. Pearson.* Edited by Jessie H. Goodman. Los Angeles: Scraps
 of California VI, 1961.
 pp. 56, port., f-map   350 copies

Of the 350 copies printed, 150 were prepared as a keepsake for the Zamorano Club. The introduction by John Barlett Goodman states that this is "virtually unknown to collectors." Pearson went south of Death Valley and entered California by way of Cajon Pass. Interesting descriptions of those he met along the way tend to make this a vibrant and entertaining narrative.

 Ref.: P-1537

362. [1850] **(Peltier, Jerome, Ed.)** a
Journal of Edmund Cavileer Hinde. Fairfield, Wash.: Ye Galleon Press, 1983.
pp. 82

Hinde was twenty years old when he started for California. After reading of Hinde's traveling problems, one may surmise that he may have bitten off more than he could chew. He stayed in California only a few months before heading back East.
Ref.: none

363. [1853] **Pengra, Charlotte Stearns** a
Diary of Mrs. Bynon J. Pengra (Charlotte Emily Stearns) Kept by Her on a Trip across the Plains from Illinois to Oregon in 1853. Eugene, Oreg.: Lane County Historical Society, (1959).
pp. 56, port., wraps, ptd. on rectos only.
rpt.: 1966, same

Mrs. Pengra traveled from Illinois to Oregon in 1853 with her husband Bynon. This is a well written account of the journey, giving a good firsthand view of the heavy work load accorded a woman on the trail. The diary concludes abruptly, as her family approaches the Willamette Valley, with the statement ". . . I am all used up. Dark times for we folks."
Ref.: none

364. [1849] **Perkins, Elisha Douglass** a
Gold Rush Diary. Being the Journal of Elisha Douglass Perkins on the Overland Trail in the Spring and Summer of 1849. Edited by Thomas D. Clark. Lexington, Ky.: University of Kentucky Press, 1967.
pp. 206, e-maps, maps, illus.

Perkins "packed" overland to Sacramento with mules, thus avoiding what he felt were many of the troubles others encountered because of their reliance on wagons. Still, Perkins does meet with his share of difficulties along the trail. Once in California, one of his close traveling companions, Samuel E. Cross, succumbs in the diggings, impressing Perkins with a premonition of what his own fate might be. Failing at the mines he loathes, Perkins worked as captain of a steamboat, but he died a few years later before he could ever return home. A well written, well edited narrative.
Ref.: none

365. [1857] **Perrie, George W.**   bbb
*Buckskin Mose; or Life From the Lakes to the Pacific . . . Written
by Himself . . .* (George W. Perrie). Edited by C. G. Rosen-
berg. New York: Henry L. Hinton, Publisher, 1873.
pp. 285 and 2 (ads.), 12 illus.
rpt.: 1890, pp. 288
Author George Perrie delivers a blow-by-blow account, including an
ample quantity of dialogue, of an overland journey with a group called
the Crim party. Possibly fiction. Cowan says of it: "A curious mixture
of desperate exploits and sentiment" (p. 82).
Ref.: C-p. 82, G-3252, H-P242

366. [1847] **Pettit, Edwin**   aa
Biography of Edwin Pettit 1834–1912. Salt Lake City: Arrow
Press, N. d. (possibly 1912).
pp. 22, port.
Pettit wintered at Council Bluffs then crossed the plains to Utah in
1847. In 1849 he became involved in driving cattle to California. For
the cattle drive portion only see *Journals of Forty-Niners; Salt Lake to
Los Angeles* by Leroy R. and Ann W. Hafen, pages 293–96. *
Ref.: none
* Arthur H. Clark Co., Glendale, Calif., 1954.

367. [1846] **Phillips, William**   c
Crossing the Plains in '46. Oregon City: Courier-Herald, 1900.
pp. 32, wraps
A poem, which may be fiction, concerning the trip. Reportedly, a
copy can be found at the University of Washington. The book is very
rare, only a few copies are known, and is almost impossible to secure.
Ref.: none

368. [1849] **Pierce, E. D.**   a
The Pierce Chronicle. Edited by J. Gary Williams and Ronald
W. Stark. Moscow, Idaho: Idaho Research Foundation, Inc.,
(1975).
pp. 127, illus., photos, e-maps   3000 copies
These are the personal reminiscences of an early Idaho pioneer as
transcribed by Lou A. Larrick. Pierce gives a low key description of
his overland trip to the Sacramento Valley that occupies one chapter
of this finely printed book (pp. 13–28). Struggling unsuccessfully in
the mines until 1852, he opted for Idaho where he discovered gold
on Oro Fino Creek and had the early town of Pierce named after him.
It was the first discovery of gold in Idaho. Many interesting pictures,
a few relating to overland travel, are included.
Ref.: none

369. [1853] **Piercy, Frederick H.**   1st: d, rpt.: aaa
Route from Liverpool to Great Salt Lake Valley; Illustrated with Steel Engravings and Wood Cuts from Sketches made . . . Edited by James Linforth. Liverpool: Franklin D. Richards, 1855.
pp. 120, double columns, f-map, many plates (map size 28.5 × 46.5 cms.)
rpt.:   1959, Los Angeles, Westernlore Press
anr. ed.: in 15 monthly parts, 1854–55. Part one has a notice to subscribers; the last lists contents. (Very rare, $7,000.00 and up.)

An adventurous expedition of historical significance. Piercy started in New Orleans; visited St. Louis and Nauvoo, then journeyed over South Pass to Great Salt Lake Valley. The excellent views are highly detailed and some of the earliest representing the trail. (In some copies the Utah map is hand colored.)
Ref.: G-2501, H-I359, WC-259

370. [1850] **Pigman, Walter**   aa
The Journal of Walter Griffith Pigman. Edited by Ulla Stanley Fawkes. Mexico, Mo.: Walter G. Staley, 1942.
pp. 82, frontis port., illus., e-maps   200 copies
The Foreword says, "The age-worn diary has lain hidden away half-forgotten for over eighty years. . . ." It is the daily diary of an overland trek from Ohio to Hangtown depicting hardship on the plains and the tough life of a miner. The overland trip covers thirty or so pages and is a good narrative.
Ref.: H-P361, P-1556, W-159

371. [1852] **Platt, P. L. and N. Slater**   1st: ddd, rpt.: aa
The Travelers Guide across the Plains, Upon the Overland Route . . . Accurately Measured by Roadometer, and Describing the Springs, Streams of Water, Hills, Mountains, Camping Places . . . Chicago: Daily Journal Office, 1852.
pp. 64, f-maps, wraps
rpt.: 1963, San Francisco, pp. 59, f-map
The Everett D. Graff collection held the only known perfect copy of this notable, and quite rare, overland guide. Nelson Slater is the author of *Fruits of Mormonism.* Beautifully reprinted by Barbara Holman for John Howell Books.
Ref.: C-p. 882, G-3304, H-P417, P-1561, WC-217a

372. [1849] **Pleasants, William J.**   ccc
Twice Across the Plains. 1849 . . . 1856. San Francisco: Walter N. Brunt Co., 1906.
pp. 160, frontis port., 12 plates

A down-to-earth account of two trips across the plains; the first seeking gold, the second to bring his family to the coast. Overcoming such disasters as cholera epidemics and attacks from the Indians, Pleasants provides many interesting details about the routes, the Great Divide, and merits of some of the overland guidebooks. There is a possibility that all, or most of, the copies printed were destroyed by fire in 1906.

> Ref.: C-p. 494, G-3305, H-P421

373.   [1860]   **Porter, Lavinia Honeyman**   ccc
By Ox Team to California. A Narrative of Crossing the Plains in 1860. Oakland: Oakland Enquirer, 1910.
pp. 139, port.

One of the rarest of the modern overland narratives, each of the fifty printed copies is numbered. Although Lavinia, her husband, and young son strayed somewhat from the Oregon Trail, this adventure gains importance because it speaks of meeting with the handcart pioneers, and returning Pike's Peakers. The Porters went overland from St. Joe to Denver, but finding the area not respectable for a decent woman, they again took to the trail in July, finally arriving in Hangtown during October. Although penniless, with a young son, and unused to the rigors of such a trip, they made their way successfully. A copy sold at the Streeter Auction for $275.00 and another at the Dr. Henry W. Plath Auction in 1959 for $375.00.

> Ref.: C-p. 496, G-3325, H-P488

374.   [1852]   **Potter, Theodore E.**   aa
Autobiography of Theodore Edgar Potter. (Concord, N. H.): pvt. ptg., (1913).
pp. 228, 3 ports.

Potter treked overland in 1852 by ox team. He relates his doings in the California diggings and of other daily events. A scarce book.

> Ref.: C-p. 497, G-3333, H-P514, W-160

375.   [1859]   **(Power, Bertha Knight)**   aa
William Henry Knight, California Pioneer. N. p., 1932.
pp. 252, f-map, illus.

Knight was a friend of Samuel Clemens. This book tells of his overland trip in the chapter "Emigrant train en route to California."

> Ref.: none

376.   [1856]   **Powers, Mary Rockwood**   a
A Woman's Overland Journal to California. Edited by W. B. Thorsen. Fairfield: Ye Galleon Press, 1985.
pp. 76

The editor discovered the author of this anonymous account in 1924 when he found a book that contained letters by Mary Powers about the trip (*see* 377). This pensive journal tells of hazards of the journey, the death of the Powers' two children, and culminates with the death of the author, herself a victim of the trail.

Ref.: none

377. [1856] **Powers, W. P.**   bbb
      Some Annals of the Powers Family (with) Journal of the Trip across the Plains to California in 1856. Los Angeles, 1924.
      pp. 304, illus.

Another over the plains journal seldom seen for sale. The overland section of this book consists of some eighty pages, the remainder being, for the most part, involved with family history in Wisconsin. (*See also* 376.)

Ref.: none

378. [1847] **Pratt, Orson**   a-aa
      Exodus of Modern Israel. Salt Lake City: N. B. Lundwell, 1947.

Taken from his private journal, this is concerned with the overland journey from Nauvoo to the Great Salt Lake. This material was originally published in the *Latter Day Saints' Millenial Star* in Liverpool in 1849–50.

Ref.: WC-171

379. [1847] **Pratt, Parley**   aaa
      The Autobiography of Parley Pratt, One of the Twelve Apostles of the Church . . . Edited by His Son, Parley P. Pratt. New York: Russell Bros., 1874.
      pp. 502, 6 plates

A recounting of Pratt's busy life, including mention of his 1847 overland trip to Salt Lake City.

Ref.: H-P556

380. [1849] **Pritchard, James A.**   aa
      The Overland Diary of James A. Pritchard from Kentucky to California in 1849. Edited by Dale L. Morgan. Denver: Old West Publishing Co., 1959.
      pp. 222, port., 2 f-maps, large f-chart in pocket

This is one of the most capably researched and written overland books, about one of the earliest diarists to reach California in 1849. The included chart provides a complete summary of all known South Pass overland expeditions of the year, with dates and destinations.

Ref.: P-1590

381. [1843] **(Prosch, Thomas W.)**   bb
      McCarver and Tacoma. Seattle: Lowman and Hanford, 1906.
      pp. 198, illus. (photos)
A scarce account privately printed for friends. D. M. McCarver went
to Illinois in 1829; to Iowa in 1832; and overland to Oregon in 1843.
He tells of becoming part of the gold rush in 1848 and later tells of
the Indian wars in Oregon. Included here are McCarver's letters,
written while crossing the plains.
      Ref.: H-P635

382. [1850] **(Prosch, Thomas W.)**   b-bbb
      *David S. Maynard and Catherine T. Maynard. Biographies of
      Two of the Oregon Immigrants of 1850 . . .* Seattle: Lowman
      and Hanford, (1906).
      pp. 80, 2 ports., wraps
The preface states that, "The immigrants tired of themselves and of
each other. Stretching out these conditions for a period of five months
drove some of the participants into suicide, others into insanity, and
left many a physical wreck for whom there was no possibility of re-
covery." Included is David Maynard's day-by-day journal describing
his overland trip.
      Ref.: G-3368, H-P634

383. [1842] **Pruess, Charles**   a
      *Exploring with Fremont. The Private Diaries of Charles Pruess,
      Cartographer for John C. Fremont on His First, Second, and
      Fourth Expeditions to the Far West.* Norman: University of
      Oklahoma Press, 1958.
      pp. 162, maps, illus.
In his first two expeditions, Fremont covered the overland route to
Oregon. Pruess, writing in his diary, seemed to consider Fremont
somewhat of a windbag and an incompetent. His opinion may stem
from his not having received sufficient gratification from the energetic
and far-seeing Fremont. Whatever the case, Pruess's comments give
a down-to-earth view of the travels and in some instances are quite
amusing.
      Ref.: E-p. 136, P-1585

384. [1846] **Purcell, Polly Jane**   bb
      Autobiography and Reminiscences of a Pioneer. (Freewater, Oreg.,
      1922). (Date and place uncertain.)
      pp. 7, printed on rectos only

Polly Jane came west over the Oregon Trail in 1846 in a train guided by Joe Meek. She tells of the Whitman Massacre and early days in Oregon. By all accounts, she crossed the mountains twelve times. In all probability, a very small printing.

Ref.: G-3402

385. [1851] **(Raulston, Marion Churchill)**   aa
            Memories of Owen Humphrey Churchill and His Family. N. p.: pvt. ptg., 1950.
            pp. 93 (no pagination), photos, illus.

The book includes some genealogy of the Churchill family, plus an account of their overland trip to Oregon in 1851. The "memories" also include adventures prospecting in British Columbia, Idaho, and Oregon. A small number were printed and it is now a scarce book.

Ref.: none

386. [1850] **Read, George Willis**   aa
            A Pioneer of 1850: George Willis Read 1819–1880. The Record of a Journey Overland . . . Edited by Georgia Willis Read. Boston: Little, Brown, and Co., 1927.
            pp. 185, frontis port., 15 plates, f-map

Considered by many to be one of the best overland narratives. Read was a gentleman, blessed with feeling and understanding, and he wrote an interesting, intelligent journal of the trip. He was a member of the Jefferson-California party from Pennsylvania and the journal takes the reader from the early days of planning to their destination of Hangtown (Placerville).

Ref.: C-p. 523, G-3431, H-8420 (1954), P-1625, W-163

387. [1862] **Redfield, Francis M.**   a
            Reminiscences of Francis M. Redfield, Pioneer of Oregon and Idaho. Pocatello, 1949.
            pp. 124, frontis, wraps

Somewhat typical of the many books of old-timers' "recollections" that includes a number of things that occurred during his lifetime. Reviewed here is Redfield's overland trip to Oregon in the year of 1862.

Ref.: none

388. [1849] **Reid, Bernard J.**   a
            Overland to California with the Pioneer Line. Edited by Mary McDougall Gordon. Stanford, Calif.: Stanford University Press, 1983.
            pp. 247, e-maps, illus.

A fine printing of this recently discovered diary telling of young Reid's experiences as a member of the best known commercialized wagon train to attempt the overland trail. Much more complete than the Niles Searls diary concerning the same trip (*see* 409), this day-by-day record delivers an accurate depiction of the problems, difficulties, and trying hardships encountered by those who had paid $200.00 to be comfortably conveyed by mule train to California, and instead barely survived the ordeal. Indeed, many members didn't make it. An important overland diary and a well edited book.

Ref.: none

389. [1853] **Remy, Jules and Julius Brenchly**   Paris ed.: d,

English: ccc

Voyage au pays des Mormons. 2 vols. Paris, 1860.

pp. 432 and 544, map, 10 plates, illus.

English ed.: *Journey to the Great Salt Lake City.* 2 vols. London: W. Jeffs, 1861.

pp. 508 and 606, f-map (44 × 16¹/₂ cms.), 10 plates, illus.

In 1855 Remy traveled through the Carson Valley from San Francisco to Salt Lake. Volume two contains extracts from Brenchley's journal of his overland trip to Oregon in 1853. A Mormon bibliography is included, pp. 561–69.

Ref.: G-3461, H-R210, WC-364

390. [1847] **(Richardson), Colby, Mary E.**   a

The Story of the Richardson Family. Dalla, Oreg., 1929.

pp. 22, wraps

The Richardsons started in May of 1847 from Iowa and traveled the Oregon Trail to the Willamette Valley, arriving in October.

Ref.: none

391. [1854] **Richey, James**   c

A Trip across the Plains in 1854. (Richey, Calif., 1908).

pp. 8, wraps

This is an extremely rare narrative with only one or two copies known. Richey and his brother, from Illinois, traveled along the well known rivers of the Overland Trail: the Platte, the Sweetwater, and the Humboldt. Their destination was Downiesville.

Ref.: none

392. [1851] **Riddle, George W.**   aa
History of Early Days in Oregon. Riddle, Oreg., 1920.
pp. 74, double columns, frontis port., plate, wraps
This is a reprint of the article as it first appeared in the *Riddle Enterprise.*
Riddle emigrated to Oregon in 1851 from Springfield, Illinois. Much
of the book is on early Indian problems in Oregon.
Ref.: none

393. [1860] **Rigdon, Winfield Taylor**   bb
Crossing the Plains in 1860. Salem, Oreg., N. d.
pp. 4 (illus. title page)
This account appears in the form of a poem.
Ref.: none

394. [1852] **Riker, John F.**   ddd
*Journal of a Trip to California by the Overland Route; Containing
All the Principal Incidents of the Journey; Also a Description of
the Country, Soil, Climate, and Principal Streams and Rivers;
with a Summary of the Entire Distance from Cincinnati to San
Francisco via the Plains . . .* (Urbana, Ohio) (place uncertain),
(1855).
pp. 32
The 1982 Wagner-Camp gives a brief history of the book. Mr. George
Miles, Curator of Beinecke Library at Yale, was kind enough to supply
the year Riker made his trip. Pages 29–32 are devoted to John Sinclair,
regarding the Donners. Only one copy is known.
Ref.: H-R298, WC-268

395. [1849] **(Ritter, Mary Bennett)**   aa
More than Gold in California, 1849–1933. Berkeley: pvt. ptg.,
1933.
pp. 451
Chapter three contains excerpts from the diary of John Clifton who
left Berrien County, Michigan with twenty others for the journey to
the coast. Brief as it is, this may be the only recording of the Clifton
diary. Most of the book is drawn fom Mary Ritter's later life. Nicely
printed.
Ref.: none

396. [1849] **Roberts, Sidney**   dd
      *To Emigrants of the Gold Region. A Treatise Showing the Best
      Way to California, with Many Serious Objections to Going by
      Sea, Doubling the Cape, or Crossing the Isthmus, with the Con-
      stitution and Articles of Agreement of the Joint Stock Mutual
      Insurance Merchandising Company* . . . New Haven, 1849.
      pp. 12, wraps
Another one of the many who attempted to sway those looking for
help in choosing an overland route. Roberts's aim was to entice his
reader through the new Mormon town of Salt Lake. The first part of
this treatise was thirty-two pages in length, with two illustrations, and
was titled "An appeal to Citizens of the U.S., the Martyrdom of the
Two Prophets, Joseph and Hiram Smith. . . ."
      Ref.: none

397. [1849] **Robinson, Zirkle D.**   a
      *The Robinson-Rosenberger Journey to the Gold Fields of Califor-
      nia, 1849–50. The Diary of Zirkle D. Robinson. Edited by Francis
      Coleman Rosenberger.* Iowa City, (1966).
      pp. 26
Robinson's diary is one of the many contemporary journals passed
down through the years, from one family member to another, until it
finally found a publisher. Robinson's jottings are a typical example of
the many overland diarists who wrote in a curt, concise style—generally noting one or two line descriptions of the day's occurrences.
An attractive little book.
      Ref.: none

398. [1856] **Romney, Miles P.**   a
      Lilfe Story of Miles P. Romney. Edited by Thomas Cattam
      Romney. (Salt Lake City, 1948).
      pp. 424, ports.
He relates his experiences as one of the Mormon Handcart Pioneers
of 1856, along with happenings of his later life in Utah.
      Ref.: none

399. [1848] **Root, Riley**   dd
      *Journal of Travels from St. Joseph's to Oregon, with Observations
      of that Country, Together with a Description of California, Its
      Agricultural Interests and a Full Description of Its Gold Mines.*
      Galesburg, Ill.: Gazetteer and Intelligencer Prints, 1850.
      pp. 143, wraps (yellow)
      rpt.: 1955, Oakland, pp. 130, 500 copies

Howes says this is "one of the best overland journals, one of the few covering 1848, one of the earliest describing the California gold-fields, which he reached from Oregon, 1849." And Graff, quoting collector Webster Jones, says "Riley Root was an excellent reporter and a careful observer, both qualities that make this book one of the top four written about the overland route to Oregon."

Ref.: G-3565, H-R436, WC-189

400.   [1849]   **Royce, Sarah**   aa
A Frontier Lady. Recollections of the Gold Rush and Early California. Edited by Ralph Henry Gabriel. New Haven: Yale University Press, 1932.
pp. 144, frontis, map
This book was drawn from Sarah's diary of 1888. It was originally intended for family perusal only; the writing was encouraged by her son Josiah, a professor of philosophy at Harvard.

Ref.: G-3598, P-1702

401.   [1852]   **Rudd, Lydia Allen**   a
Women's Diaries of the Westward Journey. Edited by Lillian Schlissel. New York: Schocken, (1982).
pp. 262, frontis, map illus.
Lydia wrote a short diary "Notes by the Wayside en route to Oregon, 1852," found on pages 187 to 198 of this book by Lillian Schlissel. Lydia speaks ominously of the rapid spread of sickness that seemed, in one way or another, to affect all, including her and her husband. She ends the diary with a poem.

Ref.: none

402.   [1841]   **Sage, Rufus B.**   1st: ccc, 2nd: bbb, anr. ed.: aaa
Scenes in the Rocky Mountains, and in Oregon, California, New Mexico, Texas, and the Grand Prairies; or Notes by the Way . . . by a New Englander. Philadelphia: Carey & Hart, 1846.
pp. 303, f-map (43.5 × 59.5 cms.)
2nd ed.: 1847, Philadelphia, pp. 303
anr. ed: 1854, Philadelphia, pp. 303 & 24 (ads.), 10 plates
also: 1855, 1857, 1858
Sage was one of the earliest to travel the trail as an experience. His first jaunt was in 1841 with Lancaster P. Lupton's group to Ft. Platte, Wyoming (other ventures followed). The trip was obviously a commercial venture for Lupton. Sage's prime motivation appears to have been to obtain "adventures" for this book. His second undertaking in 1842 took him as far northwest as Ft. Hall.

Ref.: C-p. 548, G-3633, H-S16, WC-123

403. [1850] **Sawyer, Lorenzo** Ltd. ed.: bb, 1st: aaa
Way Sketches; Incidents of Travel across Plains from St. Joseph to California in 1850. Edited by Edward Eberstadt. New York: Edward Eberstadt, 1926.
pp. 126, frontis, ports. 385 copies
Of the 385 copies of this book, thirty-five were done in a limited edition on large paper. Sawyer's account was first published in Ohio newspapers and is one of the few contemporary journals of the 1850 overland journey across the plains. Sawyer became a Chief Justice of the Supreme Court of California. A scarce book.
Ref.: C-p. 570, G-3687, H-S133, P-1729, W-175

404. [1849] **(Scamehorn, Howard L.)** a
The Buckeye Rovers in the Gold Rush. Athens: Ohio University Press, 1965.
pp. 195, map, illus.
This book interweaves the diaries of two members of the "Buckeye Rovers," J. Elza Armstrong and Edwin Banks. They suffered no great problems and no casualties on their trip to the west.
Ref.: none

405. [1849] **Scarborough, A.** a
Diary of a Member of the First Mule Pack Train to Leave Fort Smith for California in 1849. Edited by Bessie Wright. Canyon, Texas, (1969).
pp. 59, wraps
Scarborough's diary was originally printed in the *Panhandle-Plains Historical Review.* Scarborough's group started in Arkansas, journeying north to follow the Platte. Unfortunately, the diary ends in Wyoming.
Ref.: none

406. [1849] **Scharmann, Hermann B.** c
Scharmann's Overland Journey to California. From the Pages of a Pioneer's Diary. Translated by Margaret H. and Erich W. Zimmerman, from *Scharmann's Landreise nach Californien.* (New York, 1905)
N. Y.: pvt. pvt. (1918).
pp. 114, frontis port., illus. 50 copies ptd.
The author started in the same party as Louis Nusbaumer and experienced some of the same hardships. Scharmann unfortunately decided to take his family with him; his wife and young daughter died shortly after completion of the long, arduous journey. Published originally in

1852 in a New York German newspaper, subsequently in book form in New York about 1905, also in German. That very scarce book usually sells in the $250.00 to $500.00 range. This, the first printing in English, is also very scarce.

Ref.: C-p. 571, G-3693, H-S149, W-177, WC-217b

407. [1852] **Scott, Harvey Whitefield** c
History of the Oregon Country, Compiled by Leslie M. Scott. Cambridge, Mass.: Riverside Press, 1924.
6 vols., plates, ports., facs.
Contains the 1852 diary of the Scott family journey to Oregon. Scott, editor of the "Oregonian" from 1877 till 1910, was fourteen when the trip was made. This is a compilation of his work.

Vol. 1. pp. 348, frontis, 11 plates, 1 map
Vol. 2. pp. 341, frontis, 10 plates
Vol. 3. pp. 352, frontis, 11 plates, 3 maps
Vol. 4. pp. 379, frontis, 11 plates, 6 maps
Vol. 5. pp. 313, frontis, 10 plates
Vol. 6. pp. 304, index
Ref.: none

408. [1863] **Scoville, Adaline Ballou** aa
Life of Adaline Ballou Scoville by Herself. Bingham Canyon, Utah, 1906.
pp. 45
Adaline traveled over the plains with a Mormon company in 1863, her mother being a member of the church. She later moved to Bannack City, Montana where she cooked for the miners. Following that, she moved many more times, stopping in towns all over the West. Perhaps because of the amount of movement in her life, her overland experiences receive little attention.
Ref.: none

409. [1849] **Searls, Niles** aaa
The Diary of a Pioneer and Other Papers. Edited by Robert M. Searls. (San Francisco, 1940).
pp. 90
Searls writes a thoughtful, dramatic diary as a passenger in Turner and Allen's ill-fated "Pioneer Line" out of Independence. He vividly records the problems of this enterprise, including poor daily mileage (sometimes only two or three miles), an intimate association with trail deaths, and the lack of foresight by those in charge (Searls reports

they left 75,000 pounds of baggage near Ft. Laramie). Death overtook as many as one out of four passengers. Indeed, taking Searls's condition upon reaching California as an example, it's a wonder as many survived as did. The intended guide for the journey was the famed mountain man Black Harris, who died of cholera a week prior to leaving. This is a scarce book done in a very limited printing.

Ref.: W-180

410. [1849] **Sedgley, Joseph**   ccc
Overland to California in 1849. Oakland: Steam Book and Job Printers, 1887.

pp. 66   25 copies ptd.

Sedgley was a member of the "Sagamore and California Mining and Trading Company." This day-by-day narrative provides a realistic and, at times, grim picture of the hardships and perils endured by the emigrants. Some idea of the diary's tone is evident in the fact that Sedgley kept a record of all the graves he passed en route. Sedgley traveled from Massachusetts, arriving at the diggings in September.

Ref.: C-p. 575, G-3723, H-S268

411. [1851] **(Sengstacken, Agnes Ruth)**   a
Destination West. Portland, Oreg.: Binford and Mort, (1942).

pp. 219

Agnes relates the story of her young mother's journey overland to Oregon, a trip which took six months to complete and caused much hardship. Her mother, married only a short time, traveled with her husband, Freeman Lockhart. Their destination, after moving about the Oregon countryside, proved to be the Coos Bay area. The book contains many interesting, and perhaps forgotten, facets of pioneer life.

Ref.: none

412. [1849] **Senter, Riley**   aa
Crossing the Continent to California Gold Fields. Exeter, Calif.: 1938.

pp. 30, port., illus.

Based on letters by Senter describing his late season adventure over the plains (he didn't reach Salt Lake City until August 25), and his later life in the Golden State. He continued west after leaving Salt Lake by way of the southern road.

Ref.: none

413. [1847] **Sessions, Patty**   a
Covered Wagon Women. Edited by Kenneth L. Holmes. Glendale: Arthur H. Clark Co., 1983.
pp. 272, frontis, f-map, errata slip
Patty, a respected midwife, tells of the experiences encountered by the Mormon party she was a member of, as they journeyed from Winter Quarter to the Salt Lake area. The diary occupies pages 165 to 185 of this well printed introductory work in a ten-volume series.
Ref.: none

414. [1849] **(Settle, Raymond W., Ed.)**   aa
March of the Mounted Riflemen. Glendale: Arthur H. Clark Co., 1940.
pp. 380, frontis, f-map, 22 plates
A reprinting of the detailed journal of Osborne Cross (*see* 112). This volume also contains the epigrammatic diary of George Gibbs, and the official report of Colonel Loring. Cross was a member of the first U.S. military expedition to travel the Oregon Trail in its entirety. This book is number three of the Northwest Historical Series issued by the Clark Co.
Ref.: none

415. [1858] **Seville, William P.**   aaa
Narrative of a March of Co. A Engineers from Fort Leavenworth, Kansas to Fort Bridger, Utah, and Return, May 6 to October 3, 1858. Washington Barracks: Press of Engineer, 1912.
pp. 46
Contains some material on the Mormon Trail and the Utah Expedition.
Ref.: G-3734, H-S300

416. [1849] **(Sexton, Mrs. Lucy Ann (Foster), Ed.)**   bb
The Foster Family, California Pioneers; First Overland Trip, 1849 . . . (Santa Barbara, Calif., 1925).
pp. 285, ports., illus.
This is the revised edition concerning the Foster family's adventures (*see* 161). The added journal here tells of a trip via Panama. This edition's price has been generally higher than the price of the first edition of 1889.
Ref.: H-F292

417. [1849] **Seymour, Ephraim S.**   ddd
      Emigrant's Guide to the Gold Mines of Upper California, Illus-
      trated With a Map. Chicago: R. L. Wilson, Daily Journal
      Office, 1849.
      pp. 104, f-map (size, 21.5 × 13 cms.), wraps
This guidebook includes nine routes by land and sea. Of the few known
copies, one is in the Bancroft Library, another at the New York Public
Library, and one at Texas Christian University at Ft. Worth.
      Ref.: H-S312, W-182, WC-173a

418. [1852] **Sharp, James Meikle**   b
      Brief Account of the Experiences of James Meikle Sharp. (Saticoy,
      Calif.) (place uncertain), 1931.
      pp. 72, ports
An account of an 1852 overland trip to Oregon. The cover has the
title *Early Recollections.*
      Ref.: H-S332

419. [1850] **Shaw, David Augustus**   aaa
      Eldorado; or, California as Seen by a Pioneer, 1850–1900. Los
      Angeles: B. R. Baumgardt, 1900.
      pp. 313, frontis, plates
Shaw first crossed the plains with the "Wild Rovers" in 1850. His
second crossing came in 1853. Much of the book deals with the life
and labors of early California.
      Ref.: none

420. [1849] **Shaw, Reuben C.**   bb
      Across the Plains in Forty-nine. Farmland, Ind.: pvt. ptg. for
      the author's family, 1896.
      pp. 200, frontis, port.
      rpt.: 1948, Lakeside Press
A record of the difficult six-month overland trip of the Mt. Washington
Mining Company from Boston to the mines. Others of this same party
were Kimball Webster and Joseph A. Stuart (*see* 452; 490). Shaw's
book offers a good picture of the hardships suffered, such as cholera,
pursuit by the Indians, and natural phenomena. Apparently, very few
were printed.
      Ref.: C-p. 580, G-3744, H-S349

421. [1850] **Shepherd, Dr. J. S.**   rpt.: aaa
*Journal of Travel across the Plains to California and Guide to the
Future Emigrant.* Racine, Wis.: Published by Mrs. Rebecca
Shepherd, 1851.

pp. 44
rpt.: 1945, Placerville, 200 copies

The doctor left Racine the fifth of March, and during the stifling
months of July and August became one of those who encountered
numerous difficulties along the Humboldt River in present-day Nevada. Even so, his wagon, horsedrawn, completed the trip; surely, as
Shepherd notes, he was one of the few who did. On reaching Placerville, August 15, he began his practice of medicine. Of the two
known copies of the first printing, one copy is in the Rollins Collection
at Princeton, the other at the Huntington Library.
Ref.: C-p. 891, H-S388, W-186, WC-204

422. [1849] **Sherwood, J. Ely**   dd
*The Pocket Guide to California; a Sea and Land Route Book,
Containing a Description of the El Dorado.* New York: J. E.
Sherwood, 1849.
pp. 98, f-map (size, 32 × 47 cms.), wraps

Howes states that the first edition had seventy-two pages and "later
copies include advs. at rear carrying paginat. to 80 in some copies, to
98 in others." Besides being a rare book this is obviously a unique
guide as it also claims overland travel by air is possible in a new
invention, the "revoidal spindle."
Ref.: C-p. 583, H-S409, W-187, WC-173b

423. [1852] **Shipp, Ellis Reynolds**   a
The Early Autobiography and Diary of Ellis Reynolds Shipp, M.D.
Edited by Ellis Shipp Musser. N. p., (1962).

pp. 292

Edited by Mrs. Musser from her mother's diary. Ellis Shipp traveled
from Iowa to Utah in 1862. In 1876 she developed an interest in
medicine, went to Philadelphia to study, and became a specialist in
obstetrics.
Ref.: none

424. [1846] **Shively, John M.**   dd
*Route and Distances to Oregon and California, with a Description
of the Watering Places, Crossings, Dangerous Indians . . .* Washington, D.C.: Wm. Greer, Printer, 1846.
pp. 15, wraps
rpt.: *Overland in 1846 . . . ,* Dale Morgan, ed., 1963,
Georgetown, pp. 734–42 of Vol. 2.

Three photostatic copies were known to be made of this exceedingly
rare pamphlet. It gives many safety hints along with a mileage chart
from Independence to Astoria. This guidebook was based on Shiveley's
1842 journey.

Ref.: C-p. 584, WC-124

425.   [1848]   **Simpson, Henry**   1st: dd, rpt.: b-bb
                *The Emigrant's Guide to the Gold Mines. Three Weeks in the
                Gold Mines, or Adventures with the Gold Diggers of California
                in August, 1848* . . . New York: Joyce and Co., 1848.
                pp. 30 (plus 2 ad. pages), map (not issued in all copies)
                rpt.: 1978, Haverford, Pa., pp. 81 (includes one full page
                      facs.), prologue and epilogue by Franz R. Dykstra.
Dykstra says the original guide is a "classic exercise in imaginative
misinformation."
Simpson was a member of Stevenson's regiment, and claimed to have
spent three weeks working in the mines. The guide contains his "Adventures with the Gold Diggers," and a brief description of the country
in general.

Ref.: C-p. 589, G-3788, S-497, W-189

426.   [1850]   **Slater, Nelson**   d
                *Fruits of Mormonism; or a Fair and Candid Statement of Facts
                Illustrative of Mormon Principles* . . . Coloma, Calif.: Harmon
                & Springer, 1851.
                pp. 94
Slater went over the plains by way of the Platte River and Salt Lake
City, his party wintering at the latter. After arriving in the Carson
Valley the next spring, the party held a meeting. The result was that
200 members signed resolutions, and sent a message to Congress,
stating bitter complaints about the Mormons, charging them with
treason, larceny, murder, etc. They asked for the abolition of the Utah
Territorial Government and gave a warning to emigrants planning to
journey that way. Excessively rare, this is the first book printed at
Coloma, where gold in California was first discovered.

Ref.: C-p. 591, G-3814, H-S542, W-190, WC-205

427.   [1862]   **Smedley, William**   c
                Across the Plains in '62. Denver, (1916).
                pp. 56, illus., map   50 copies
Smedley's interesting day-by-day diary tells of still another instance
where the author, quite sickly during his lifetime, develops into a
robust pioneer once on the trail. His story of traveling overland to

Oregon with a wagon and usually only one companion, is a strong argument for those who lean toward the belief that small parties fared the best. His two worst enemies were mosquitoes and Indians. This rare account runs the gamut of price ranges, having recently been offered for sale at prices ranging from under $100.00 to a high at $500.00.

Ref.: G-3820, H-S566

428.   [1850]   **Smith, C. W.**   aa
Journal of a Trip to California across the Continent from Weston, Missouri to Weber Creek, California in 1850. Edited by R. W. G. Vail. New York: Cadmus Book Shop, (1920).

pp. 79

This is a small book containing adventures of some interest. Smith tells of incidents with the Indians, ferry boats, Wisconsin wagons, and, among other things, lack of food.

Ref.: C-p. 592, G-3836, P-1821, W-191

429.   [1847]   **Smith, Elizabeth Dixon**   a
Covered Wagon Women. Edited by Kenneth L. Holmes. Glendale: Arthur H. Clark Co., 1983.

pp. 272, frontis, f-map errata slip

An engaging diary found in Volume I (pp. 111–55), of the series titled *Covered Wagon Women.* Elizabeth traveled a rough road to Oregon caring for seven children and a husband who was taken sick just after reaching their land of promise. Upon his demise she describes her existence: ". . . how comfortless is that of a widow's (sic) life espesily (sic) when left in a strange land without money or friends and the care of seven children." (*See also* 172.)

Ref.: none

430.   [1845]   **Snyder, Jacob R.**   a
Diary of Jacob R. Snyder Written when Crossing the Plains to California in 1845. San Francisco: California Pioneers Society, 1931.

pp. 36, wraps

Snyder was a member of one of the first organized overland expeditions to California. Caleb Greenwood guided the train. Snyder speaks of meeting Thomas Fitzpatrick, Joseph Walker, Antoine Roubidoux, and Gen. Stephen Kearny.

Ref.: none

431. [1850] **Sortore, Abram**   bb
     Biography and Early Life Sketch of the Late Abram Sortore In-
     cluding His Trip to California and Back. Alexandria, Mo., 1909.
     pp. 10, double columns, pictorial cover
Sortore started near Keokuk, Iowa and traveled to Hangtown. A very
scarce pamphlet, with only a few copies known to exist.
     Ref.: C-p. 894

432. [1852] **Stabaek, Tosten K.**   a
     An Account of a Journey to California in 1852. Northfield,
     Minn.: Studies and Records, 1929.
     pp. 99–124 (numbered thus)
An interesting account. Translated from Norwegian by Einar I. Hau-
gen. The rush to the gold diggings as seen through the eyes of a
Norwegian moving overland with a Norwegian party. He tells of incidents along the way and of taking the Lassen cutoff. The clear
recounting of the events for this narrative, done some forty years later,
emphasize the strength with which the journey was blazed into the
memory of those making the trip. This was first published in *Aabok*
Nr. 14 for Numedalslaget, 1928.
     Ref.: none

433. [1849] **Stansbury, Howard**   bb
     An Expedition to the Valley of the Great Salt Lake . . . Phila-
     delphia: Lippincott, Grambo & Co., 1852.
     pp. 487, map, 57 plates, 2 f-maps in separate vol.
     other eds.: Exploration . . . of the Valley . . . (Sen. Exec.
                 Doc. 3) same date, imprint, and collation.
               : Same, except ptd. by Armstrong, Wash.
               : 1853, House of Rep., pp. 495, same maps and
                 plates, but inferior imprint.
               : 1852, London, same as Philadelphia
Stansbury's work took him over a good part of the trail, where he
met, talked with, and saw the same features as the emigrants. He,
along with his subordinate, J. W. Gunnison, explored most of the
area around the Great Salt Lake. A difficult book to find in fine
condition.
     Ref.: G-3947, H-S884, WC-219

434. [1852] **Starbuck, Edith**   aa
     Crossing the Plains. Nashville: Southern Publications, (1927).
     pp. 224, frontis, f-map, plates

A story revolving around the overland trip of the Ingalls, Lyman, and Hayden families to Oregon in 1852 containing an abundance of obviously fictionalized conversation. Somewhat difficult to locate.

Ref.: none

435. [1850] **Starr, Jeremiah**   bb
A *California Adventure and Vision. Prose and Poetry.* Cincinnati, 1864.

pp. 102

Starr crossed the plains from Indiana to Hangtown with four companions in 1850, and later traveled widely throughout the diggings. He devotes much of his narrative to the miners' everyday lives.

Ref.: H-S902

436. [1849] **Steck, Amos**   a
Forty-niner: His Overland Diary to California; a Pioneer Coloradan. Edited by Nolie Mumey. Denver: The Range Press, 1981.

pp. 187, photos   200 copies

Another wonderfully printed book from Mr. Mumey; in this one he rescues from near obscurity a fine overland narrative. Steck was in the middle of the forty-nine rush, and relates a mordant picture of the travelers he meets and the helter-skelter life that he becomes a part of. The book consists mostly of his lengthy diary. Added to it are short chapters surrounding his life.

Ref.: none

437. [1850] **Steed, Thomas**   b
The Life of Thomas Steed from His Own Diary. (Salt Lake City: pvt. ptg., 1935)

pp. 43, plates, wraps (green)

This little known diary contains a colorful and interesting account of Steed's travels from Liverpool to Nauvoo, his subsequent trek to Salt Lake City, his adventures during the years 1844 to 1850 prior to the overland journey, and his later experiences in the far west. Chad Flake in his *A Mormon Bibliography* cites this, or an earlier issue, as being done in Farmington, Utah, possibly in 1911.

Ref.: G-3956, H-S915

438. [1850] **Steele, John**   b
Across the Plains in 1850. Chicago: Caxton Club, 1930.

pp. 274, frontis, f-map   350 copies

This well known overland adventure was edited by Joseph M. Schafer and was originally printed in the *Lodi Valley News* in Lodi, Wisconsin in the year 1899. Steele's sharp eye and educated mind (he was training to become a teacher), produced a first-class, detailed narrative that relates his adventures in traveling over the plains. He was also the author of *Steele's Guide to California*. A most attractive book.

Ref.: H-S923, W-195

439. [1854] **Steele, John**   dd
The Traveler's Companion through the Great Interior. A Guide for the Road to California, by the South Pass in the Rocky Mountains . . . Galena: Power Press of H. H. Houghton & Co., 1854.

pp. 54, wraps   5 copies known
Author of *Across the Plains in 1850*, this guide was primarily for those going by way of South Pass and interested in "Sublett's" (sic) and Headpath's" (sic) cutoffs.

Ref.: C-p. 612, G-3965, H-S925, WC-244

440. [1849] **Steele, Oliver G.**   16th: c, rpt.: aaa
Steele's Western Guidebook, and Emigrant's Directory; Containing Different Routes through the States of New York, Ohio, Indiana . . . with an Appendix Containing the Routes to Oregon and California. Sixteenth Edition. Buffalo: Oliver G. Steele, 1849.

pp. 72, 2 maps (sizes, 35 × 48 cms., 10 × 23.5 cms.)
rpt.: Buffalo, N. d., pp. 72, same imprint
This edition was the first to include any information on the far western trails. Popularity of this book may have arisen in part from the inclusion of the two maps.

Ref.: H-S927, WC-173c

441. [1849] **Stemmons, John**   dd
The Journal of Maj. John Stemmons of Rocheport, Mo. . . . Noted Down in the Shape of Familiar Letters to His Friends, and Embracing Every Incident connected with His Trip to California Over the Plains Last Year. St. Louis: Fisher and Bennett, 1850.

pp. ?, wraps
The information for this entry was taken from Wagner-Camp-Becker. That bibliography should be consulted should the reader be so fortunate as to discover this almost unknown book about overland travel. No copy is known.

Ref.: WC-192a

442. [1856] **(Stenhouse, Thomas B. H.)** aaa
The Rocky Mountain Saints: A Full and Complete History of the Mormons . . . London: Ward, Lock, and Tyler, 1874.
pp. 761 and 24 (ads.), illus.
Of primary interest here is "Mr. Chislett's" narrative, pages 312 to 332. He tells of the tragedies encountered by the 1856 Mormon Handcart Companies in their attempt to cross the plains to Salt Lake City.
Ref.: none

443. [1856] **Stenhouse, Mrs. T. B. H.** aa
"Tell It All." The Story of Lifes Experiences in Mormonism. (sic) Hartford: A. D. Worthington Co., 1874.
pp. 623, frontis, illus.
This early exposé of Mormon life includes a long letter describing the experiences of Mary Burton, a friend of the author and member of the tragic handcart company led by James G. Willie. A vivid description is told of the trials that were encountered by this party of over 400, one sixth of which, according to the writer, was buried along the way. She mentions that the company which followed fared even worse, burying one of every four members. Mrs. Stenhouse's journey overland to Salt Lake City is barely alluded to.
Ref.: none

444. [1849] **Stephens, Lorenzo Dow** bb
Life sketches of a Jayhawker of '49 . . . Actual Experiences of a Pioneer Told by Himself in His Own Way. (San Jose: Nolta Bros.), 1916.
pp. 68, 6 plates, wraps 300 copies ptd.
Stephens accompanied William Manly as one of the "Jayhawkers" in the party. A "Jayhawker," it appears, was an unattached man in the group. He provides an interesting narrative, including his version of the trek through Death Valley.
Ref.: C-p. 613, E-p. 152, G-3972, H-S941, P-2498

445. [1853] **Stewart, Agnes (Warner)** a
The Diary of Agnes Stewart (with) A Letter of Elizabeth Young Stewart Warner. Eugene, Oreg.: Lane County Historical Society, 1959.
22 (part one), pp. 5 (part two), wraps, ptd. on rectos only
Agnes was a young girl of 21, traveling with the party that became known as the "Lost Wagon Train." Her diary, which carries only periodic entries towards the end of the trip, is disappointing as it adds little knowledge to this little known episode of trail literature. Also included is an unfinished and unmailed letter, regarding the trip, by her sister Elizabeth.
Ref.: none

446. [1844] **(Stewart, George R.)** a
Opening of the California Trail. The Story of the Stevens Party from the Reminiscences of Moses Schallenberger as Set Down for H. H. Bancroft about 1885, Edited and Expanded by Horace S. Foote in 1888, and Now Edited with Introduction, Notes, Maps, and Illus. by George R. Stewart. Berkeley and Los Angeles: University of California Press, 1953.
pp. 115, map, 14 photos, illus.
The best book on the Stevens-Murphy party of 1844 and Moses Schallenberger's lone sojourn through the winter at what was to become Donner Lake. This was the winter before the Donner party reached it. What there is of Schallenberger's account is printed here.
Ref.: none

447. [1859] **Stockton, William J.** aaa
The Plains over; the Reminiscences of William J. Stockton. Written by Ralph Leroy Milliken. Los Banos, Calif.: Enterprise Print, 1939.
pp. 55, port., wraps
Stockton's story includes the account of an overland journey and the early history of Los Banos. Reportedly, only a few copies of this book were printed.
Ref.: none

448. [1848] **Stout, Hosea** aa
On the Mormon Frontier: the Diary of Hosea Stout, 1844–1861. 2 vols. Edited by Juanita Brooks. Salt Lake City, 1965.
pp. 769, illus., ports., maps
This work is one of the best sources of Mormon history. Stout was at Winter Quarters on the Missouri from Fall of 1846 to Spring of 1848. He includes in his diary a rare account of the happenings there. Stout went overland to Utah in 1848. Later, although lacking any previous experience in law, he was named "States Attorney." His diary therefore contains not only views of the people but also a close look at early Utah politics.
Ref.: none

449. [1850] **Street, Franklin** d
California in 1850, Compared with what It Was in 1849, with a Glimpse at Its Future Destiny. Also a Concise Description of the Overland Route, from the Missouri River, by the South Pass . . . Cincinnati: R. E. Edwards & Co., 1851.
pp. 88, frontis, 2 plates

Street obtained at least part of his information on the overland trails from guidebooks of the day. The number of pages includes the frontis and two other plates. A difficult book to find.

Ref.: C-p. 620, G-4007, H-S1071, WC-206

450. [1852] **Stuart, Granville**   1st: bb, rpt.: aa
Forty Years on the Frontier. 2 vols. Cleveland: Arthur H. Clark Co., 1925.
pp. 272 and 265, frontis port., photos
rpt.: 1960, Glendale, 2 vol. in 1

This is one of the best books on early Montana history written by a well educated pioneer. On pages 23 to 56 of volume one, Stuart tells of his father's overland trip in 1849 and of his own in 1852. A scarce book.

Ref.: H-1096

451. [1849] **Stuart, Joseph A.**   d
My Roving Life. A Diary of Travel and Adventures by Sea and Land, during Peace and War. 2 vols. Auburn, Calif.: ptd. by the author, 1895.
pp. 203 and 229, 20 maps and plates   50 copies ptd.

Graff says, "Dale Morgan noted that Stuart started overland in 1849 with the 'Granite State Company' which united with the 'Mount Washington Company.' " R. C. Shaw was also a member of the Granite State Company, as was Kimball Webster. Only fifty copies were reported printed.

Ref.: C-p. 622, G-4021, H-S1102

452. [1860] **Stucki, John S.**   aaa
Family History: Journal of John S. Stucki, Handcart Pioneer of 1860; across the Plains to Utah and South to St. George. Salt Lake City, (1932).
pp. 164   250 copies ptd.

After distributing the books to all family members only fifteen copies were left. Only these fifteen were made available to the public. Stucki relates the hardships as a handcart pioneer, and of his early days in Utah. The overland diary is a good one and covers the first seventy-five pages of vol. 1. Some of his reminiscences include herding sheep with Jacob Hamblin, pioneering in Santa Clara County, and road building.

Ref.: none

453.   [1845] **Swasey, William F.**   bb
       The Early Days and Men of California. Oakland: Pacific Press,
       1891.
       pp. 406, port., 2 plates
Swasey crossed the plains in 1845, going to work for Sutter. The "early
days and men" are mostly concerned with 1846–47.
       Ref.: C-p. 627, G-4047, H-S1167, W-203

454.   [1843] **Talbot, Theodore**   a
       *The Journals of Theodore Talbot, 1843 and 1849–52 with the
       Fremont Expedition of 1843 and with the First Military Company
       in Oregon Territory 1849–1852.* Portland: Metropolitan Press,
       1931.
       pp. 153
An important supplement to Fremont's narrative, providing many
noteworthy details not recorded elsewhere. Talbot talked with a number of the overland pioneers of 1843 and during the expedition often
traveled in company with Fitzpatrick and Carson.
       Ref.: H-T13

455.   [1853] **Tarbell, J.**   ddd
       *The Emigrant's Guide to California; Giving a Description of the
       Overland Route from the Council Bluffs . . . by South Pass, to
       Sacramento City . . .* Keokuk: Whig Book and Job Office,
       1853.
       pp. 18, wraps
Graff tells of the discovery of three copies in the closet of Horace
Ayer's widow. These copies were purchased by Eberstadt. Edwin Carter,
an ex-newspaperman, had earlier received his own copy from the
widow which he later sold to Goodspeed. Wagner-Camp-Becker contains a bit of information about the book itself. Only a few copies are
known to exist.
       Ref.: G-4068, WC-233

456.   [1849] **Taylor, Joseph (William G. Underbrink)**   bb
       *A Journal of the Route from Ft. Smith, Arkansas to California
       in the Year 1849. With a Full Account of the Trail, Necessary
       Equipment, and Many Other Interesting Facts as Experienced on
       Route.* Bowling Green: Job Office, 1850.
       pp. 15, wraps
This is a phony narrative. Has enough substance to carry it through
the years as a factual account. Therefore, it is still of interest to many
in this area.
       Ref.: G-4084

457. [1847] **(Taylor, L. J. Orr)**   aa
Life History of Thomas Orr, Jr., Pioneer of California and Utah.
N. p., 1930.
pp. 51, ports., plates, wraps
Orr was a member of the Mormon exodus of 1847. He gives a detailed
version of life in Winter Quarters, the journey over the plains to Salt
Lake, and his trek over the Sierra Mountains to California. He was
a noted pioneer of California's early days.
Ref.: none

458. [1845] **Tethrow, Captain Sol.**   a
Captain Sol. Tethrow, Wagon Train Master: Personal Narrative
of His Son . . . Who Crossed the Plains to Oregon, in 1845 . . .
and Whose Father Built the Fourth House in Portland. By Fred
Lockley. Portland, Oreg., N. d.
A brief journal by the leader of a company of sixty-six wagons traveling
from "St. Joe" to Oregon. The other wagon trains that left St. Joe
during 1845 were led by A. Hackleman, W. G. T'Vault and Samuel
Parker. T'Vault had John Waymire as assistant. According to the
narrative, two wagon trains left Independence in 1845 as well. One
was guided by Presley Welch, with Joel Palmer and Samuel A. Barlow
as assistants. The other train was under the charge of Samuel Hancock.
However, Hancock is also listed as a cattle driver in the Tethrow train.
Unless there were two Samuel Hancocks, it would appear that Hancock began the trip as a cattle driver in Tethrow's train, and proving
his worth along the trail, found himself at the head of a group of
emigrants at the journey's conclusion. The Tethrow pamphlet also
includes a "Census of the Oregon Emigration."
Ref.: none

459. [1845] **Tethrow, Solomon**   a
The Organizational Journal of an Emigrant Train of 1845, Cap-
tained by Solomon Tethrow, with an Account of the Wagon Train
. . . by Fidelia March Bowers. Eugene, Oreg.: Lane County
Pioneer Historical Society, 1960.
pp. 29, frontis, typescript on rectos only
A picture of Tethrow and a family genealogy is included.
Ref.: none

460. [1850] **Thissell, G. W.**   bb
Crossing the Plains in '49. Oakland: pvt. ptg., 1908.
pp. 176, frontis port., 11 plates, illus.
Thissell did not actually start his travels until the spring of 1850,
when, with an ox-team, and as a member of the very small Chambers

train, he began his long overland journey. He arrived in California in September of that year. His narrative is interspersed with anecdotes from many old pioneers.

Ref.: C-p. 634, G-4124, H-T160, W-206

461. [1849] **Thomas, Martha Pane**   a
       Daniel Stillwell Thomas Family History. Salt Lake City, 1927.
       pp. 64, ports.

This narrative was written during the years 1883 to 1890. She tells of her conversion to the Mormon faith and of her trip over the plains to Utah. She, as did other women, speaks of being concerned with the popularity of polygamy.

Ref.: none

462. [1849] **Thomason, Jackson**   a
       *From Mississippi to California / Jackson Thomason's 1849 Over-
       land Journal.* Edited by Michael D. Heaston. Austin: Jenkins
       Book, 1978.
       pp. 124, frontis port.

Thomason's day-by-day diary of his journey from Mississippi to the gold diggings. He tells of being one of many who signed a pact as a member of the California Exploring and Mining Company. The pledge of this group, as with many other like groups, appeared to be a bonding of loyalties. Thomason writes, however, that selfishness and bickering caused each member to spurn his vows, and the pact was dissolved, the company disbanded, in Salt Lake City. Throughout the trip, Thomason questions his own motives in joining the rush. His obvious reasons may be due, to some extent, to a guilty conscience, as his wife was quite sick when he departed.

Ref.: none

463. [1849] **Thompson, George Alexander**   c
       *Handbook to the Pacific and California, Describing Eight Different
       Routes.* London: Simpkin and Marshall, 1849.
       pp. 108, map (22 × 18.5 cms.), plate

Another very difficult book to find concerning the various ways to reach the Pacific Coast.

Ref.: H-T194, WC-173d

464. [1852] **Thompson, William**   aa
       Reminiscences of a Pioneer. San Francisco, 1912.
       pp. 187, frontis, illus.

This book was issued in a small printing. Thompson crossed the plains in 1852 to the Willamette. However, the retelling of his overland journey occupies only the first ten pages of the book. The reminiscences are rather more important for their view of the Northern California and Oregon Indian wars as seen by (Col.) Thompson.

Ref.: C-p. 637, G-4138

465. [1852] **Thomson, Origen** cc
Crossing the Plains, Narrative of the Scenes, Incidents and Adventures Attending the Overland Journey of the Decatur and Rush County Emigrants to the "far-off" Oregon, in 1852. Greensburg, Ind.: Orville Thomson, Printer, 1896.

pp. 122, wraps

Thomson left Indiana as a member of a group called the Crawford party. The book contains a list of most of the members of this party of 111 emigrants.

Ref.: G-4140, H-T216

466. [1846] **Thorton, Jessy Q.** c
Oregon and California in 1848 . . . Including Recent and Authentic Information on the Subject of the Gold Mines of California . . . 2 vols. New York: Harper & Bros., 1849.

pp. 393 and 379, illus., f-map (size, 47.5 × 41 cms.)
rpt.: 1855, 1864 (same collation)

Thornton arrived in Oregon in 1846. His book has maintained a good reputation as a source of reliable information about the times. In addition, he gives one of the first written accounts of the Donner tragedy.

Ref.: C-p. 638, G-4143, H-T224, WC-174, Z-74

467. [1862] **Tourtillott, Jane Gould** a
Women's Diaries of the Westward Journey. Edited by Lillian Schlissel. New York: Schocken, (1982).

pp. 262, frontis, map, illus.

Jane Gould's short (pages 219 to 231), and sporadically kept diary, "Touring from Mitchell, Iowa, to California, 1862," offers a woman's view of the 1862 Indian scare to the emigration. She speaks of knowing whether she would still be alive come morning. Her husband's health deteriorated along the trail and he died not long after reaching the Santa Clara Valley.

Ref.: none

468. [1849] **(Trowbridge, Mary E. Day)** aaa
Pioneer Days: The Life-story of Gershom and Elizabeth Day by M. E. D. Trowbridge. Philadelphia: American Baptist publication society, (1895).

pp. 160, frontis port.

The Reverend Mr. Day went over the plains to California in 1849. He was killed by Indians a few years later. A scarce book apparently written by the daughter.

Ref.: C-p. 644, H-T359

469.   [1847]   **Trubody, William Alexander**   a
William Alexander Trubody and the Overland Pioneers of 1847.
Edited by Charles L. Camp. Printed by Lawton Kennedy.
pp. 22, frontis, wraps (gray)

Trubody tells of his overland excursion by ox team. He started at Dover, Mississippi and reached Sutter's Fort in 1847. This was re-printed by Lawton Kennedy from the *California Historical Society Quarterly.*

Ref.: none

470.   [1859]   **True, Charles Frederick**   a
Covered Wagon Pioneers. Edited by Sally Ralston True. Mad-ison: College Printing Co., (1966).
pp. 107, illus., maps, wraps

True traveled from Owatonna, Minnesota to Placerville. He had an eventful trip, having somewhat difficult confrontations with Indians along the way, a tenuous time crossing the deserts of Nevada, and entering California by the Carson route. Paher in his Nevada Bibli-ography calls this "As exciting a tale as was ever concocted by Hol-lywood . . . ," giving a good argument to doubt the authenticity. In any event it's a colorful narrative.

Ref.: P-1993

471.   [1852]   **Turnbull, Thomas**   aaa
. . . *Travels from the United States across the Plains to California.*
Madison: Published for the Society, 1914.
pp. 151–225 (numbered thus), maps, wraps

A detailed account edited by Paxson and Thwaites. Taken from the "Proceedings of the State Historical Society of Wisconsin, 1913." Turnbull emigrated to Hangtown from the Chicago area. He tells of traveling by way of the Mormon Trail on the north side of the Platte.

Ref.: G-4207

472.   [1852]   **Udall, David**   aa
Arizona Pioneer Mormon; David King Udall, His Story and His Family 1851–1938 Written in Collaboration with His Daughter, Pearl Udall Nelson. Tucson: Arizona Silouettes, 1959.
pp. 314, e-maps, ports., illus.

Udall, an Englishman, crossed the plains to Utah during 1852. As a Mormon priest, he aided those Mormons who settled in Arizona. Also included here is some of the early Mormon history in Utah.

Ref.: none

473. [1850] **Udell, John** cc
Incidents of Travel to California, across the Great Plains; Together with the Return Trips through Central America and Jamaica; to which are Added Sketches of the Author's Life. Jefferson, Ohio: Printed for the Author, at the Sentinel Office, 1856.
pp. 302, frontis port. (not in all copies)
The author, a Baptist minister, was almost fifty-five years old when he undertook his first overland journey in 1850. He went again in 1852 and 1854 and all trips were to California. The diary information concerning his trips only occupies about one-third of the book, the rest relates other experiences and secondary information.

Ref.: C-p. 649, G-4231, H-U3, W-213

474. [1858] **"Utah"** a
To Utah with the Dragoons and Glimpses of Life in Arizona and California, 1858–1859. Edited by Harold D. Langley. Salt Lake City: University of Utah Press, (1974).
pp. 230, maps, illus.
Consists of letters by a writer known only as "Utah." The letters were first published in 1858–59 in a Philadelphia newspaper, the *Daily Evening Bulletin.* "Utah" writes of Chimney Rock and other historical points along the trail, as he traveled with a recruit detachment to Camp Floyd, Utah to participate in the Mormon "War." Intelligently and perceptively written. The editor supplies much information at the conclusion of the book to allow the reader the opportunity to deduce the true identity of the mysterious "Utah."

Ref.: WC-346b

475. [1849] **Wade, Almira** a
The Jayhawkers' Oath and Other Sketches, by William L. Manly. Edited by Arthur Woodward. Los Angeles: Warren F. Lewis, 1949.
pp. 168, large f-map, illus.
Pages 157 to 165 contain the account of the Wade family, "Across the Plains in 1849," one of the families that might have perished in Death Valley had Manly and Rogers not been able to return in time. This was originally contributed to the Plainfield, Illinois, *Enterprise* some years ago by Mrs. Edward Burrel of Santa Clara who was a close friend.

Ref.: none

476. [1858] **Wadsworth, William**   ddd
              The National Wagon Road Guide from St. Joseph and Council
              Bluffs . . . via South Pass of the Rocky Mountains to California
              Containing Minute Descriptions of the Entire Route . . . San
              Francisco: Whitton, Towne & Co., Printers and Publishers,
              1858.
              pp. 160, frontis, f-map (size, 13.5 × 45.5 cms.)
Wadsworth wrote this from experience, having made a number of trips
overland. He tells of some of the experiences met with while traversing
the plains in this clearly written guide. Streeter called this the "most
satisfactory" of the overland guides. Only four copies are known to
exist.
              Ref.: C-p. 665, G-4502, H-W3, WC-313

477. [1852] **Waggoner, George**   aaa
              Stories of Old Oregon. Salem, Oreg.: Statesman Publishers,
              1905.
              pp. 292, 19 plates
A personal narrative of Waggoner's trip overland from Winchester,
Iowa, to Oregon. He speaks of observations in the mines and the
campaign against the Snake Indians.
              Ref.: G-4503

478. [1862] **Waite, Catherine Van Valkenburg**   aa
              Adventures in the Far West and Life Among the Mormons. Chi-
              cago, 1882.
              pp. 311
Catherine tells of traveling overland to Salt Lake City in 1862, and,
as the title indicates, she relates stories of her life among the Mormon
folks. Flake in his *A Mormon Bibliography* calls this fiction.
              Ref.: none

479. [1849] **Walton, Daniel**   ccc
              The Book Needed for the Times, Containing the Latest Well-
              Authenticated Facts from the Gold Regions; Also, a Geographical
              and Historical View of California, with the Different Routes, by
              Land and Water, and Their Difficulties. Boston: Stacy, Rich-
              ardson & Co., 1849.
              pp. 32
This also includes a poem by Walton concerning California. A very
scarce book that advises the interested to stay home. Cowan gives the
height of this publication as 22.8 cms.
              Ref.: C-p. 668, H-W77

480. [1853] **Ward, Dillis B.**   1st: bbb, rpt.: aa
Across the Plains in 1853. Seattle: Bull Bros., (1911).
pp. 55, frontis port., wraps
rpt.: 1945, Wenatchee, Wash., World Pub.
Howes says that Ward "Started from Arkansas, followed the Santa Fe
Trail to Colorado, then north to the Overland Trail and Oregon."
Many hardships were met with on this unusual path to the Dalles.
Ref.: G-4530, H-W94

481. [1853] **Ward, Harriet Sherill**   a
Prairie Schooner Lady. Edited by Ward G. DeWitt and Florence
Stark DeWitt. Los Angeles: Westernlore Press, 1959.
pp. 180, maps, illus.
Ward emigrated from Wisconsin to Indian Valley, California. She
wrote an intelligent account of the Indians, Mormons, prairies, storms,
and campfire scenes encountered along the trail. Her attitude is perhaps best illustrated by this thought: "You may possibly infer from this
remark that I am becoming weary of this mode of life but indeed, my
dear children, were you all with us and our horses fresh it would
notwithstanding all its hardships be to me a perfect pleasure trip.
There is so much variety and excitement about it, and the scenery
through which are constantly passing is so wild and magnificently
grand that it elevates the soul from earth to heaven and causes such
an elasticity of mind that I forget that I am old. Indeed I sometimes
feel as I should take the wings of the morning and fly away" (p. 132).
One of the best overland diaries.
Ref.: P-2091

482. [1849] **Ware, Joseph E.**   1st: dd, rpt.: a
*Emigrant's Guide to California, containing Every Point of Infor-
mation for the Emigrant—Including Routes, Distances, Water,
Grass, Timber, Crossing of Rivers, Passes, Altitudes, with a Large
Map of Routes, and Profile of the Country . . .* St. Louis, Mo.:
Published by J. Halsall, (1849).
pp. 55, f-map (size, 35 × 118 cms.)
rpt.: 1932, Princeton, pp. 64, map, 2 plates
The best of the early guides to California, even though, according to
Wheat, Ware wrote it before traversing the route. It's almost certain
many of the original copies were worn out from use by those emigrating. Van Allen Bradley says of the last two copies sold at auction,
both lacked the map. Selling prices recorded show this book com-
manded $1000.00 (1948) and $500.00 (1968).
Ref.: C-p. 669, G-4538, H-W104, W-220, WC-175

483. [1853] **Washburn, Catherine Amanda S.**   a
      *The Journal of Catherine Amanda Stansbury Washburn, Iowa to
      Oregon in 1853.* Eugene, Oreg.: Lane County Historical So-
      ciety, 1967.
      pp. 30, ports., wraps, ptd. on rectos only
Ten years after arriving in Oregon, Mrs. Washburn rewrote her pen-
cilled diary in ink. The original diary done while crossing the plains
is here, as are a large number of additional comments excerpted from
the rewritten work. These insertions add a smattering of color and
interest to this crudely kept record.
      Ref.: none

484. [1855] **Waters, L. M.**   aa
      Account of a Trip across the Plains in 1855. San Francisco:
      Society of California Pioneers, 1929.
      pp. 20, maps, wraps
A brief telling of a journey from Belleville, Iowa, to the mines.
      Ref.: none

485. [1849] **Watson, William J.**   ddd
      *Journal of an Overland Journey to Oregon, Made in the Year
      1849.* Jacksonville, Ill.: T. R. Roe, 1851.
      pp. 48, wraps
The only known copy is reportedly in the library at Harvard. Highly
notable as it is one of the few published journals of the 1849 journey
to Oregon.
      Ref.: H-W174, WC-207

486. [1851] **(Watt, Roberta Frye)**   aa
      Four Wagons West, the Story of Seattle. Portland, (1931).
      pp. 390, illus.
This tells the story of Watt's mother's overland trip from Cherry Grove,
Illinois, to the Oregon Territory. It also makes use of the diary kept
by her grandfather, Arthur Denny.
      Ref.: none

487. [1852] **Waugh, Lorenzo**   1st: aaa, rpt.: a
      Biography of Lorenzo Waugh. Oakland: Pacific Press, 1883.
      pp. 311, port., illus.
      rpt.: 1884, San Francisco
Waugh gives a personalized narrative of his experiences on the plains
and on his later life in the Golden State.
      Ref.: C-p. 672, G-4561, H-W181

488. [1852] **Wayman, Dr. John Hudson**   a
            A Doctor on the California Trail; the Diary of Dr. John Hudson
            Wayman from Cambridge City, Indiana, to the Gold Fields in
            1852. Edited by Edgely Woodman Todd. Denver: Old West
            Publishers, (1971).
            pp. 152, large f-map, illus.

Wayman's strikingly boorish and rather pompous attitude permeate
his diary. Still, in between his entries, which seem to alternate between
exhilaration and dejection, he writes an interesting description of the
trip to the mines.
A nicely printed book from Fred Rosenstock's Old West Publishing
Company of Denver.
            Ref.: none

489. [1849] **Webster, Kimball**   aaa
            The Gold Seekers of '49. A Personal Narrative of the Overland
            Trail and Adventures in California and Oregon from 1849 to
            1854. Manchester, N. H.: Standard Book Co., 1917.
            pp. 240, frontis port., 15 plates

Webster, a surveyor, writes of traveling along the Platte, reaching
Oregon, and later going to California, in what appears to be a hastily
written diary. He was a member of the same company as Joseph A.
Stuart and R. C. Shaw.
            Ref.: C-p. 673, G-4571, W-222

490. [1854] **Welch, John Allen**   bb
            Personal Memoirs of John Allen Welch in Narration Form including
            an Overland Trip From Iowa to California in 1854 . . . Hutch-
            inson, Kans., 1920.
            pp. 125, 2 ports., wraps

A difficult book to find, probably printed in a small edition for friends
and family.
            Ref.: none

491. [1853] **West, Calvin B.**   aa
            Calvin B. West of the Umpqua. Edited by Reginald R. and
            Grace D. Stuart. Stockton: California Historical Foundation,
            1961.
            pp. 114, frontis port., illus., map   250 copies

The Umpqua is one of the picturesque river valleys of southwestern
Oregon. West gives a sketchy description of his overland trip there,
focusing his diary more on his activities as teacher, and later a missionary. He died of cholera while bringing his family west on the boat
Sierra Nevada. This limited printing describing early Oregon history
was nicely done by Lawton Kennedy.
            Ref.: none

492. [1852] **West, George Miller**   cc
      An Autobiography. Los Angeles, 1937.
      pp. 87, wraps
Reportedly there were only seven copies of this typed manuscript made.
The author went overland in 1852 as a member of the Pierce Butler
wagon train. Later he wrote his memoirs of the trip to Oregon's Polk
County, and his experiences as a miner in Oregon and Northern
California. Also included are ten letters written home to relatives from
other members of the Butler Company.
      Ref.: none

493. [1859] **West, Simeon H.**   aaa
      Life and Times of Simeon H. West. Leroy, Ill., (1908).
      pp. 298, illus.
The relating of his adventures, including an overland trip in 1859 to
California, and his enthusiastic spiritual beliefs.
      Ref.: G-4598, H-W281

494. [1852] **Whipple-Haslam, Mrs. Lee**   bb
      *Early Days in California, Scenes and Events of the '50s As I
      Remember Them.* Jamestown: Mother Lode Magnet, (1923).
      pp. 34, plate, wraps
The author was a little girl when her parents made the journey overland
and eventually stopped near Sonora, California. She relates incidents
involving Indians and tells about how Mark Twain once resided in
her mother's boarding house.
      Ref.: C-p. 679, H-W342

495. [1852] **White, Thomas**   a
      To Oregon in 1852. Letter of Dr. Thomas White. Edited by
      Oscar O. Winther. Indianapolis: Indiana Historical Society,
      1964.
      pp. 37, wraps
A description of his journey from La Grange, Indiana, over the Oregon
Trail to the Willamette Valley. This is actually a long letter written
to a friend giving his opinions of the Indians he met along the way
and a description of living in the Valley.
      Ref.: none

496. [1849] **Wilkens, James F.**   a
      *An artist on the Overland Trail; the 1849 Diary and Sketches of
      James F. Wilkens.* Edited by John Francis McDermott. San
      Marino, 1968.
      pp. 143, 50 sketches, e-maps

To create an immense "Moving Mirror of the Overland Trail" a St. Louis painter, James Wilkens, joined the spring caravan for the road west to the gold fields. He made 200 preliminary sketches for the panorama and kept a record of the trip. The importance of this diary's contribution to the history of the overland period is reinforced by the fifty sketches, all that remain of the 200. The three-reel canvas he prepared enjoyed an enthusiastic reception, showing the Rockies, Chimney Rock, Devil's Gate, Steamboat Spring, Fort Kearney, Fort Laramie, and Fort Bridger, the unending stream of emigrants, wagons, terrifying ascents and descents, and the sublime views.

Ref.: none

497. [1843] **(Wilkes, George)**   1st: d, rpt.: c, Eng. 1st: cc, Eng. rpt.: bb

The History of Oregon, Geographical and Political . . . to Which Is Added a Journal of the Events of the Celebrated Emigrating Expedition of 1843; Containing an Account of the Route from Missouri to Astoria . . . New York: William H. Colyer, 1845. pp. 127, map (size, 21 × 28 cms.), errata

Eng. ed.: 1846, London, pp. 160, with many changes including title, *An Account and History of the Oregon Territory . . .*

Eng. rpt.: same imprint, date, and collation

This contains the 1843 journal of the Oregon emigration kept by Peter Hardeman Burnett (*see* 66; 210), one of the contemporarily printed records of the transcontinental migration during that year. The book was reprinted in Philadelphia in 1849.

Ref.: G-4657, H-W419, WC-119

498. [1841] **Williams, Joseph**   1st: ddd, rpt.: aa-aaa

Narrative of a Tour from the State of Indiana to the Oregon Territory, in the Years 1841–2. Cincinnati: J. B. Wilson, Printer, 1843.

pp. 48

rpt.: 1921, New York, pp. 95, 250 copies ptd. (12 on long paper)

Williams, a sixty-four-year-old minister at the time of his narrative, was a member of the Bidwell-Bartleson party until they branched off for California. The Reverend was such a colorful commentator on his experiences that he may have provided later authors with a character model. (See "Brother Weatherby" in *The Way West,* by A. B. Guthrie, Jr.)

Ref.: G-4682, H-W471, WC-105

499. [1853] **Williams, Wellington**
      The Traveller's and Tourist's Guide through the United States,
      Containing the Routes of Travel. Philadelphia: Lippincott,
      Grambo & Co., 1853.
      pp. 216, f-map in color (size, 26.8 × 23.2 cms.)
Reported to contain an interesting description of the route from St.
Joseph to Oregon. Drawn in 1851, possibly 1852, the map is one of
the earliest to delineate "Washington Territory." No guide for pricing
was found for this book.
      Ref.: G-4687, W-235

500. [1849] **Wilson, Luzena S.**   aa
      Luzena Stanley Wilson '49er: Memories Recalled Years Later for
      Her Daughter Correnah Wilson Wright. Oakland: Mills College,
      1937.
      pp. 61, illus.   500 copies ptd.
Mrs. Wilson dictated her reminiscences to her daughter in 1881,
relating her overland crossing from Missouri to Sacramento. She also
spent some time in Nevada City and was a pioneer of Vacaville.
      Ref.: none

501. [1849] **Wistar, Isaac Jones**   1st: bbb, 2nd ed.: aa
      Autobiography of Isaac Jones Wistar 1827–1905. 2 vols. Phil-
      adelphia: Wistar Institute, 1914.
      pp. 341 and 191, f-map, 2 plates   250 copies ptd.
      2nd ed.: 1937, Philadelphia, pp. 528, f-map, 6 plates
The first edition is rather difficult to locate. Wistar's narrative of his
journey over the Humboldt Sink to the gold areas is well told and
quite entertaining, especially the vignettes, such as when the Indians
almost get him. The overland portion covers fifty or so pages of the
book. In 1937, Harper and Brothers published a "first edition" of 530
pages, port., f-map, and illus., New York and London.
      Ref.: C-p. 692, H-W598, P-2191, W-234

502. [1849] **Wolverine Rangers**   a
      The Gold Rush Letters from the Wolverine Rangers to the Mar-
      shall, Michigan "Statesman," 1849–1851. Mount Pleasant, 1974.
      pp. 154   487 copies
Assorted members of the large company of Wolverine Rangers sent
letters back reporting their progress. Even though they started apparently well organized and in agreement, they disbanded, as so many
other companies did, before reaching the destination. The story is a
fine example of the saying that the best and worst are soon brought
to the fore under duress and trial.
      Ref.: none

503.   [1851]   **Wood, Elizabeth**   a
       Journal of a Trip to Oregon 1851. Eugene: Koke-Chapman,
       (1926).
       pp. 11, wraps
Reprinted from the *Oregon Historical Quarterly,* March, 1926. First
printed in the Peoria "Republican" on January 30, 1852, and February
13, 1852. It ended, "To be continued." Apparently no more was
published.
       Ref.: none

504.   [1850]   **Wood, John**   1st: ddd, rpt.: ccc
       *Journal of John Wood, as Kept by Him while Traveling from
       Cincinnati to the Gold Diggings in California, in the Spring and
       Summer of 1850 . . .* Chillicothe: Press of Addison Book-
       walter, 1852.
       pp. 76, wraps
       rpt.: 1871, Columbus, Nevin & Myers, pp. 112
The reprint, or second edition, is almost as rare as the first edition.
Wagner knew of only one copy of the first printing (his own). Since
that time only two or three more have been located. The Wood party
started as a group of seventy-two and ended as two. Many died from
cholera or other causes, the rest splintered to make their own way.
The journal, perhaps the most pessimistic of all overland diaries, is
noted for its entries depicting bad luck, hardships encountered, and
the example of just how bad the journey could get.
       Ref.: C-p. 693, G-4732, H-W633, WC-220

505.   [1852]   **Woodhouse, John**   a
       John Woodhouse, His Pioneer Journal. Salt Lake City: James
       Mercur, 1952.
       pp. 88
Woodhouse made his way from St. Louis to Salt Lake City in 1852.
He became a well traveled Mormon speaker who was asked by the
Church not to dwell so much on polygamy.
       Ref.: none

506.   [1853]   **Woodworth, James**   a
       *Diary of James Woodworth, across the Plains to California in
       1853.* Eugene, Oreg.: Lane County Historical Society, 1972.
       pp. 61, port., wraps, ptd. on rectos only
Woodworth's journey begins in St. Louis and culminates five months
later in the diggings in California. His day-by-day diary records his
route: along the Platte, through South Pass to Salt Lake City, and

over the Nevada deserts. He tells of the death of people and animals, although his party made it through without the devastation others experienced. Two of his close traveling companions died soon after reaching the coast.

Ref.: none

507. [1849] **Woolley, Lell H.**   b
California, 1849–1913 or the Rambling Sketches and Experiences of Sixty-four Years' Residence in that State, by L. H. Woolley. Oakland: Dewitt & Snelling, 1913.

pp. 48, frontis port., wraps

Only a few copies of this book were printed. Woolley joined the first mule train of Turner and Allen's Overland Company leaving Independence in May, during the peak of the gold rush. He writes of going overland and also of his part as a member of the San Francisco vigilantes.

Ref.: C-p. 695, G-4745

508. [1850] **Wooster, David**   a
The Gold Rush Letters of David Wooster from California to the Adrian, Michigan, Expositor. Mount Pleasant, 1972.

pp. 85   487 copies ptd.

A quick journey by the man who started the *Pacific Medical Surgical Journal* in 1857.

Ref.: none

509. [1849] **(Wyman, Walker, Ed.)**   a
California Emigrant Letters. New York: Bookman Association, 1952.

pp. 177, illus.

Contains letters from 1849 and 1850 overlanders that for the most part were published in the *Missouri Republican.* "Boone Emigrant" and "Miflin" are just two examples of the host of contributors who tell the story of their experiences on the trail, and later in the diggings.

Ref.: none

510. [1847] **Young, Brigham**   dd
General Epistle from the Council of the Twelve Apostles, to the Church of Jesus Christ of Latter-Day Saints Abroad, Dispersed throughout the Earth . . . Given at Winter Quarters, Omaha Nation, West Bank of the Missouri River, near Council Bluffs . . . Florence, Nebr. or St. Louis, (1847) (place and date uncertain).

pp. 8

Also published in Liverpool in 1848. This rare pamphlet contains an account of the pioneer party which left Nauvoo in February, 1846, an account of the building of Winter Quarters, and the story of 143 Mormon pioneers and their trip from April 14, 1847 until their arrival in the Great Salt Lake Valley.

Ref.: G-715, WC-160

511. [1847] **Young, John R.**   b
Memoirs of John R. Young, Utah Pioneer of 1847. Written by Himself. Salt Lake City: The Deseret News, 1920.

pp. 341, 4 ports., plates

Young began his trip overland at Nauvoo, continued to Winter Quarters, and to Utah in 1847. Later in his life he helped lead other Mormon followers to the Salt Lake Valley. Young, who was the son of Lorenzo Dow, speaks honestly about his plural marriages.

Ref.: G-4794, H-Y29

512. [1847] **Young, Lorenzo Dow**   a
Biography of Lorenzo Dow Young. Salt Lake City: Utah Historical Quarterly, 1946.

pp. 191, f-map, 15 plates

The first twenty or so pages give points of Mormon history. The remainder of the book concerns the diary of Lorenzo Young, who was the brother of Brigham Young. This diary presents a full history of the Mormon movements, including the overland traveling to the Great Salt Lake. The biography was written by James Amasa Little, utilizing many excerpts from Young's diary. Interesting reading.

Ref.: none

513. [1850] **Zumwalt, Solomon**   a
The "Biographa of Adam Zumwalt" by His Son, Solomon Zumwalt, Who Came to Oregon in 1850. Eugene, Oreg.: Lane County Historical Society, 1959.

pp. 25 and 9, port., ptd. on rectos only

Solomon records here the history of his father, which includes experiences with Daniel Boone. Upon completion of the "Biographa" of his father, he relates the account of his trip on the overland trail. His spelling is quite bad and at times takes a moment to decipher, which can interrupt the flow of the journal. He decided to spend the winter with the Mormons in Salt Lake City, finishing his trip in 1851.

Ref.: none

Appendix A

Red Herrings

514.   **Aldrich, Lorenzo D.**   1st: ddd, rpt.: aaa
A Journal of the Overland Route to California. Lansingburgh,
N.Y.: Alex. Kirkpatrick, 1851.
pp. 48
rpt.: 1950, Los Angeles, pp. 95, map
Aldrich traveled to San Diego by the southern route in 1849. This
rare account is the second recorded westerly trip across Arizona, following James O. Pattie's personal narrative of the early 1830s. Aldrich
died two weeks after returning home and this diary was published
posthumously.
Ref.: G-29, H-A109, WC-194

515.   **Baker, Mrs. Sarah Schoonmaker**
*The Children of the Plains; a Story of Travel and Adventure from
the Missouri to the Rocky Mountains.*
Most certainly a work of fiction.
Ref.: none

516.   **Baldridge, M.**   aa
*A Reminiscence of the Parker H. French Expedition through Texas
. . . in the Spring of 1850.* Los Angeles: pvt. ptg., 1959.
pp. 52, f-map   300 copies ptd.
The best account of this famous story of overland travel across the
southern part of the country. The problems, misery, and frustrations
are here revealed much more emotionally than in the better known
book by William Miles. This volume is nicely printed as "Scraps of
California IV."
Ref.: none

517.   **Bennett, William P.**
            The First Baby in Camp. A Full Account of the Scenes and
            Adventures during the Pioneer Days of '49.
Concerned with early mining days in California and the early days of
stagecoaches.
            Ref.: G-263

518.   **Beschke, William**   dd
            The Dreadful Sufferings . . . of an Overland Party of Emigrants
            to California . . . St. Louis: Barclay & Co., 1850.
            pp. 60, frontis, 4 plates, wraps
            anr. ed.: same with 71 pages (also eds. of 70 & 72 pages)
It seems no final priority has not yet been established as to which is
the first printing. This writing is taken from the diary of George Adam,
one of the travelers, and is, according to Howes, probably a concoc-
tion.
            Ref.: C-p. 51, G-11, H-B396, WC-179

519.   **Bigham, Rev. R. W.**
            California Goldfield Scenes: Selections from Quien Sabe's Gold-
            field Manuscripts . . .
A fictionalized account.
            Ref.: H-B444

520.   **Bonner, Geraldine**
            The Emigrant Trail.
Done in 1910, this is a western novel.
            Ref.: none

521.   **Brooks, J. Tyrwhitt**
            Four Months among the Gold-finders in Alta, California.
This fictionalized account, done in 1849, once accepted as fact, was
written by Henry Vizetelly.
            Ref.: G-4494, H-V134

522.   **Brooks, Noah**
            The Boy Emigrants. Illustrations by Thomas Moran and W.
            S. Sheppard.
A western novel from 1877.
            Ref.: none

523.   **Brown, James S.**
Life of a Pioneer, Being the Autobiography of James S. Brown.
Salt Lake City: George Q. Cannon and Sons, 1900.
pp. 520, 7 illus.
Brown enlisted in the Mormon Battalion, traveled to California in
1846 and was present when gold was discovered at Sutter's Mill. (See
California Gold, an Authentic History of the First Find, J. S. Brown,
1894; Oakland)
Ref.: none

524.   **Cairns, Mary Lyons**
The Olden Days.
Published in 1954 this deals mostly with Colorado.
Ref.: none

525.   **Canfield, Chancy L.**   aa
The Diary of a Forty-niner.
This diary, from the year 1906, begins while Canfield was in the
diggings.
Ref.: C-p. 104, G-571, H-C111

526.   **Cardinell, Charles**
Adventures on the Plains. 1922, San Francisco, California: His-
torical Society, 1922.
pp. 15, wraps
Relates the tale of traveling the southern route with the Parker H.
French party.
Ref.: G-582

527.   **Carson, James H.**
Early Recollections of the Mines and a Description of the Great
Tulare Valley.
This is not an overland narrative.
Ref.: C-p. 107, G-604, H-C183

528.   **Cedarholm, Caroline**
A Narrative of the Dangerous Journey of Mrs. Caroline Cedar-
holm, the Norwegian Missionary . . .
This is a narrative of a journey to Arizona.
Ref.: none

529. **Cheney, Joseph Warren** aa
      From a Soldier's Pen. Selected Articles from the Published and Unpublished Manuscripts of Joseph Warren Cheney. (Keosauqua, Iowa, 1918) (place, date uncertain).
      pp. 49, frontis port., wraps
      Cheney took the southern route with the same emigrant group as John Udell. Pages 18 to 62 carry an account of the Rose party, of which they were members.
      Ref.: none

530. **Christman, Enos**
      One Man's Gold; the Letters and Journals of a Forty-niner.
      Traveled west via the boat "Europe."
      Ref.: none

531. **Churchill, Charles**
      Fortunes Are for the Few.
      The route used was via Panama.
      Ref.: none

532. **Clark, Austin**
      Reminiscences of Travel, 1852–65.
      Narrative of travel by way of the Isthmus.
      Ref.: C-837, G-729, H-C429

533. **Clark, C. P. and H. E.**
      Two Diaries . . .
      Both traveled to Denver. Published in 1962.
      Ref.: none

534. **Clarke, Asa B.** cc
      Travels in Mexico and California: Comprising a Journal . . . by way of . . . the Country of the Apaches, and the River Gila . . .
      Boston: Wright & Hasty's Steam Press, 1852.
      pp. 138
      Clarke's travels took him through Mexico. He reached the mines by traveling the Gila Route to the Los Angeles area, and from there, heading north.
      Ref.: C-p. 128, E-p. 35, G-746, H-C451, WC-210

535. **Coit, Daniel Wadsworth**
      Digging for Gold—without a Shovel.
      Coit crossed Mexico to San Blas. Printed in 1967.
      Ref.: none

536. **Cole, Cornelius** aaa
Memoirs of Cornelius Cole, Ex-Senator of the United States from California. New York: McLoughlin Bros., 1908.
pp. 354, port.
Cole, in traveling over the plains, gives the reader a realistic view of the Santa Fe Trail.
Ref.: C-p. 134, G-799, H-C565

537. **Cole, Major William L.**
California: Notes of an Overland Trip to the Pacific Coast with Observations. . . .
Cole went by rail over the recently completed Transcontinental line.
Ref.: C-p. 135, H-C569

538. **Cook, Elliot Wilkinson**
Land Ho! The Original Story of a Forty-niner.
Published in 1935. Cook sailed with the Niagara & California Mining Co.
Ref.: none

539. **Crumpton, H. J. and W. B.** b
The Adventures of Dr. H. J. Crumpton during His Efforts to Reach the Gold Fields in 1849. Montgomery, Ala.: 1912.
pp. 238, 2 ports.
The doctor journeyed from Ft. Smith to California.
Ref.: C-p. 841, G-937, H-C937

540. **Damon, Samuel Chenery**
A Trip from the Sandwich Islands to Lower Oregon and Upper California . . .
This was reprinted as *A Journey to Lower Oregon and Upper California* in 1927 by the Grabhorn Press. Damon arrived by boat.
Ref.: C-p. 155, G-994, H-D44

541. **Davis, Stephen C.**
California Gold Rush Merchant.
Davis arrived in California by way of Panama.
Ref.: none

542. **De Smet, Pierre J.**
Oregon Missions and Travels Over the Rocky Mountains, 1845–46 . . . Published in 1847.
De Smet performed missionary work.
Ref.: H-D286, WC-141:1

543.   **Dexter, A. Hersey**
              Early Days in California.
       Contains a report of a voyage on the "Susan Drew."
              Ref.: C-p. 168, G-1077, H-D312

544.   **Dore, Benjamin**
              Journal of Benjamin Dore 1849–1850.
       A voyage with the Bancor Trading and Mining Co.
              Ref.: none

545.   **Dougal, William H.**
              Off for California . . . Gold Rush Artist . . .
       Dougal traveled by sea.
              Ref.: none

546.   **Douthit, Mary**
              The Souvenir of Western Women.
       This book contains short incidents from the lives of some of Oregon's
       pioneer women.
              Ref.: none

547.   **Dye, Job Francis**
              Recollections of a Pioneer.
       The author recalls a journey through New Mexico to California.
              Ref.: none

548.   **Edwards, E. S.**
              Trailing the Campfires.
       This is concerned with the Bozeman Trail.
              Ref.: none

549.   **Evans, George W. B.**
              Mexican Gold Trail; the Journal of a Forty-niner.
       Edited by Glenn S. Dumke, this book details Evans's journey through
       Mexico. Published in 1945.
              Ref.: none

550.   **Field, Stephen**
              *Personal Reminiscences of Early Days in California with Other
              Sketches.*
       A journey to California by way of Panama.
              Ref.: C-p. 208, G-1315, H-F117

551.   **Gardiner, Howard C.**
*In Pursuit of the Golden Dream; Reminiscences of San Francisco
and the Northern and Southern Mines, 1849–1859.*
Edited by Dale L. Morgan. Gardiner arrived by way of Panama.
Ref.: none

552.   **Green, Robert B.**   a
*On the Arkansas Route to California in 1849. The Journal of
Robert B. Green, Lewisburg, Pennsylvania.* Lewisburg, 1955.
pp. 87, e-maps
Traveled via Santa Fe, the Gila and Colorado Rivers, to Los Angeles.
Green had a tough time on the trail and anticipated life in California
as being even worse.
Ref.: none

553.   **Griffen, John S.**   aa
*A Doctor Comes to California. The Diary of John S. Griffen,
Assistant Surgeon of Kearny's Dragoons, 1846–1847* . . . Edited
by George Walcott Ames Jr. San Francisco: California His-
torical Society, 1943.
pp. 97, frontis port., 4 maps
A journey by the southern route. Griffen was one of the few to give
a good description of the route and only one of the two to give a
firsthand account of Kearny's historic march to San Diego from Santa
Fe. The foreword is by George D. Lyman, author of *George Marsh,
Pioneer, The Saga of the Comstock Lode,* and others.
Ref.: none

554.   **Gunn, Lewis C. and Elizabeth L.**   bb
Records of a California Family: Journals and Letters . . . Edited
by Anna Lee Marston. San Diego: pvt. ptg., 1928.
pp. 279, frontis, 13 plates   300 copies
Contains the account of Lewis Gunn's trip to the California mines in
1849 and the 1851 voyage around the Horn by his wife Elizabeth.
Howes says the plate facing p. 276 is often missing. This was reprinted
in 1974 (N. p.) in an issue of 1000 copies.
Ref.: C-p. 254, G-1688, H-M324

555.   **Hale, Richard Lunt**
The Log of a Forty-niner . . .
A voyage to San Francisco is chronicled here. Published in 1923.
Ref.: none

556.   **Hall, Marshall R.**
              Storm of the Old Frontier.
A fictional story, done in 1927, of an 1850 overland journey.
              Ref.: none

557.   **Hall, William Harrison H.**
              The Private Letters and Diaries of Captain Hall; an Epic of an
              Argonaut in the California Gold Rush.
Edited by Eric Schneirsohn. Hall journeyed by boat from Boston.
              Ref.: none

558.   **Hammond, I. (Isaac) B.**
              Reminiscences of Frontier Life.
This book, published in 1890, along with the much expanded second
edition published in 1904, are occasionally seen in booksellers' catalogs
described as "a trip across the plains." The author does travel on the
plains, and in doing so relates some fascinating stories. However, in
neither edition is there an overland journey.
              Ref.: G-1760, H-H142

559.   **Hammond, John**   aaa
              To California in 1849. Chicago: P. F. Pettibone, 1890.
              pp. 90, 3 ports.
The book is actually titled *John Hammond. Died May 28, 1889, at His*
Home, Crown Point, N. Y. . . . He went to the coast by way of Santa
Fe.
              Ref.: G-1781, H-H147

560.   **Hanson, J. M.**
              The Trail to Eldorado.
Done in 1913, this book tells of traveling the wagon road from Ft.
Benton.
              Ref.: none

561.   **Harris, Benjamin**   a
              The Gila Trail. The Texas Argonauts and the California Gold
              Rush. Edited by Richard Dillon. Norman: University of Okla-
              homa Press, (1960).
              pp. 175, map, port., illus.
From southern Texas to the gold diggings in California.
              Ref.: none

562. **Heap, Gwinn H.**   ccc
Central Route to the Pacific, from the Valley of the Mississippi to
California: Journals of the Expedition of E. F. Beale . . . and
Gwinn Harris Heap, from Missouri to California in 1853 . . .
Philadelphia: Lippincott, Grambo, and Co., 1854.
pp. 136, 13 plates, map (size, 17.5 × 87 cms.)
Includes some outstanding descriptions of the Southwest landscape
seen about them.
Ref.: C-p. 276, G-1837, H-H378, WC-235

563. **Helms, Ludvig Verner**
Pioneering in the Far East, and Journeys to California in 1849 . . .
An account of Helm's journey to San Francisco from Singapore. First
published in 1882.
Ref.: none

564. **Hill, Emma**
A Dangerous Crossing and What Happened on the Other Side.
A journey to Colorado in 1864.
Ref.: G-1887, H-H481

565. **Hovay, Frederic William**
. . . the Overland Journey of the Argonauts of 1862.
The journey was from Ft. Garry to British Columbia.
Ref.: none

566. **Johnson, Oliver**
Following the Trail to the Hidden Gold.
First published in 1914. The trip was by boat via Panama.
Ref.: none

567. **Kingsley, Nelson**
Diary of Nelson Kingsley, a California Argonaut of 1849.
He reached California around the Horn.
Ref.: C-p. 331

568. **Knower, Daniel**
The Adventures of a Forty-niner. An Historic Description of Cal-
ifornia, with Events and Ideas of San Francisco and Its People in
Those Early Days.
Knower journeyed by boat.
Ref.: C-p. 334

569.   **Lane, Joseph**
              *Biography of Joseph Lane, "Not Inappropriately Styled by His
              Brother Officers and Soldiers, 'The Marion of the War,'" by
              Western.* Washington: Congressional Globe Office, 1852.
              pp. 40, wraps
Lane traveled the Gila Route during the winter of 1848–49. When
he arrived in Oregon, sometime in March, only six of the original
twenty-two men were with him.
The first edition lists the author as "Western" (see Wagner-Camp).
Another edition, as cited by Howes and Graff, lists the author as
"Westerner" with a reference in the title to Lane's governorship of
Oregon.
              Ref.: G-3149, H-L65, WC-216

570.   **Lockwood, Charles B.**   bbb-c
              My Trip to California in 1850; Written Sixty Years Later. Day-
              tona, Florida, (1910) (date uncertain).
              pp. 16
Lockwood was a member of the Parker H. French Company. This
account is a quite rare version of the disastrous undertaking, not
recorded by Howes, Graff, Cowan, etc.
              Ref.: none

571.   **Lowe, Percival G.**
              *Five Years a Dragoon ('49 to '54) and Other Adventures on the
              Great Plains.*
This is an account of travels along the Santa Fe Trail.
              Ref.: G-2550, H-L526

572.   **McCall, Ansel J.**
              Pick and Pan. Trip to the Diggings in 1849.
This diary begins at Sutter's Fort, and is the sequel to the author's,
The Great California Trail in 1849. Wayside Notes of an Argonaut.
              Ref.: C-p. 402, H-M29

573.   **McCollum, William S.**
              California As I Saw It . . .
Published in 1850, this tells of McCollum going by way of Panama.
              Ref.: none

574.   **McDonald, William John**
              Notes by a Pioneer of 1851.
McDonald was a British Columbia pioneer. Printed in 1915.
              Ref.: none

575.
McKnight, George S.
California 49er. Travels from Perrysburg to California.
He reached the coast by traveling through Mexico.
Ref.: C-p. 873, G-2632, H-M145

576.
McNeil, Everett
The Boy Forty-niners or Across the Plains and Mountains to the Gold-Mines of California in a Prairie Schooner.
This is a work of fiction.
Ref.: none

577.
McNeil, Samuel
McNeil's Travels in 1849 to, through, and from the Gold Regions . . .
Published in 1850, this recounts a journey to California from Mazatlan.
Ref.: none

578.
Mayre, George Thomas Jr.
From '49 to '83 in California and Nevada . . .
Tells of a trip by way of Panama.
Ref.: C-p. 417

579.
Megquier, Mary Jane
Apron Full of Gold.
Edited by Robert Glass Cleland. She traveled via Panama.
Ref.: none

580.
Miles, William   1st: dd, rpt.: aa
Journal of the Sufferings and Hardships of Capt. Parker H. French's Overland Expedition to California . . . Chambersburg, Pa.: Valley Spirit Office, 1851.
pp. 24, wraps   7 known copies
rpt.: New York. (250 copies) 1916.
French led the first gold rush expedition across Texas. This chaotic affair is probably the most written about journey overland by those taking a southern route.
Ref.: G-2791, H-M597, WC-202

581.
M'Ilvaine, William Jr.
Sketches of Scenery and Notes of Personal Adventure . . .
M'Ilvaine went to California via Mexico.
Ref.: none

582.   **Moellhausen, Baldwin**   d
                        *Diary of a Journey from the Mississippi to the Coasts of the
                        Pacific . . . 2 vols.* London: Longman, Brown, Green, Long-
                        man & Roberts, 1858.
                        pp. 353 and 397, map, 11 plates in color, illus.
Moellhausen traveled with the Whipple Expedition and gives perhaps
the best account of it. This diary was originally printed in German as
Tagebuch einer reise vom Mississippi nach den kusten der Sudsee and
currently sells for about twice the cost of the above edition.
                        Ref.: G-2849, H-M713, WC-305

583.   **Mooso, Josiah**   bbb
                        *The Life and Travels of Josiah Mooso. A Life on the Frontier
                        among Indians and Spaniards, Not Seeing the Face of a White
                        Woman for Fifteen Years.* Winfield, Kans.: Telegram Print,
                        1888.
                        pp. 400, frontis port.
In his bibliography on the Santa Fe Trail, Rittenhouse reports pages
192 to 205 are concerned with Mooso's trip over that trail. Apparently,
he later continued on to the coast. As Mooso is disturbingly indefinite
about when events happen, his trip could have been accomplished
anytime in the '50s.
                        Ref.: C-p. 440, G-2885, H-M784

584.   **Myrick, Thomas S.**
                        *The Gold Rush, Letters of Thomas S. Myrick from California to
                        the Jackson, Michigan, American Citizen 1849–1855.*
Myrick traveled to the west via the Isthmus. This was published in
1971.
                        Ref.: none

585.   **Osbun, Albert G.**
                        To California and the South Seas.
This 1966 book concerns travel by way of Panama.
                        Ref.: none

586.   **Pancoast, Charles**   aa
                        A Quaker Forty-niner . . . Edited by Anna Paschall Hannum.
                        Philadelphia: University of Pennsylvania Press, 1930.
                        pp. 402, illus., e-map
Pancoast was a member of the small group of forty-niners that sought
to reach the mines through the southern part of the country. He speaks
of being guided by James Kirker.
                        Ref.: G-3180

587.   **Payson, George**
         Golden Dreams and Leaden Realities. By Ralph Raven.
A boat was utilized to transport Raven (Payson) to his golden dreams.
         Ref.: H-P153

588.   **Perrine, Henry E.**
         A True Story of Some Eventful Years in Grandpa's Life . . . Trip to California in 1849 . . .
The retelling of a jaunt through Mexico to the California mines.
         Ref.: C-p. 480, G-3255, P-245

589.   **Peyton, John Lewis**
         Over the Alleghanies and Across the Prairies.
The narrative of this account is concerned with the upper Mississippi Valley.
         Ref.: G-3266, H-P280

590.   **Pierce, Hiram Dwight**
         A Forty-niner Speaks. A Chronological Record of the Experiences of a New Yorker and His Adventures . . . from March, 1849 to January, 1851.
Published in 1930 this is a scarce account of travels by sea.
         Ref.: none

591.   **Pine, George**
         Beyond the West . . .
This book is about Colorado. Printed in 1870.
         Ref.: H-P381

592.   **Powell, H. M. T.**   d
         The Santa Fe Trail to California 1849–52. Edited by D. S. Watson. San Francisco: Grabhorn Press, (1931).
         pp. 272, 18 plates, maps   315 copies ptd.
Fifteen of the 315 copies were done with colored plates. A very scarce and sought after overland journal and one of the finest books from the famous Grabhorn Press. It consists of a day-by-day recounting of a trip from Illinois to San Diego by way of Santa Fe.
         Ref.: H-P525

593.   **Pratt, Julius H.**
         Reminiscences, Personal and Otherwise.
Pratt journeyed to California from Panama.
         Ref.: C-p. 499, G-3345, H-P554

594.   **Purple, Edwin R.**
            In Memoriam. Edwin R. Purple. Born 1831. Died, 1879.
     A traveler to the coast by way of the Isthmus of Panama.
            Ref.: C-p. 504, G-3403

595.   **Reid, John C.**   1st: ddd
            *Reid's Tramp, or, a Journal of the Incidents of Ten Months Travel
            Through Texas, New Mexico, Arizona, Sonora, and California
            . . .* Selma: Book and Job Office, 1858.
            pp. 237
            rpt.: 1935, Austin
     Reid was First Lieutenant in Colonel Crabb's Auxiliary Expedition.
     They originated at Marion, Alabama, headed for the Gadsden Pur-
     chase to explore that territory. A rare book.
            Ref.: G-3450, H-R172, WC-307

596.   **Rose, L. J.**   aa
            L. J. Rose of Sunny Slope. Edited by L. J. Rose Jr. San Marino:
            Huntington Library, 1959.
            pp. 235, illus.
     Recounts the adventures of the Rose party of which John Udell was
     a member, and which was attacked in Arizona in 1859.
            Ref.: none

597.   **Ross, James and George Gary**
            *From Wisconsin to California, and Return, as Reported for the
            "Wisconsin State Journal."*
     This is the first published account (1869) of an overland trip entirely
     by rail.
            Ref.: C-p. 543, H-R457

598.   **Russ, C. H.**
            The Log of a Forty-niner.
     The recording of a journey to the west coast by sea.
            Ref.: none

599.   **Sawtelle, Mary P.**
            The Heroine of '49.
     This is a work of fiction.
            Ref.: C-p. 569

600.   **Seymour, Silas**
            Incidents of a Trip Through the Great Platte Valley.
     Seymour traveled to the Laramie plains.
            Ref.: G-3736, H-S315

601.   **Sheldon, Stewart Rev.**
        Gleanings by the Way.
        The story of his trip to San Francisco by sea.
        Ref.: C-p. 891, H-377

602.   **Sherwell, Samuel**
        Old Recollections of an Old Boy.
        He recalls his journey from St. Joseph to Colorado in 1864.
        Ref.: G-3756, H-S405

603.   **Smith, W. C. S.**
        Narrative of a 49-er.
        Printed in 1888. Smith went from Baja to San Diego.
        Ref.: none

604.   **Stafford, Mallie**
        The March of Empire . . . Crossing the Plains with Ox Teams.
        She reached California by way of Panama.
        Ref.: C-p. 606, G-3939, H-S864

605.   **Stillman, Jacob D. B.**
        Seeking the Golden Fleece; a Record of Pioneer Life in California
        . . .
        Stillman's account of travels from N.Y. to San Francisco by voyage.
        Ref.: C-p. 616, H-S1006

606.   **Stullken, G.**
        My Experiences on the Plains.
        This account concerns Colorado, 1861–1865.
        Ref.: G-4023, H-S1108

607.   **Sumner, Charles**
        Cross the Plains. The Overland Trip. A Narrative Lecture.
        All about taking the train overland.
        Ref.: G-4030

608.   **Swan, John A.**   aa
        A Trip to the Gold Mines of California in 1848. Edited by John
        A. Hussey. San Francisco: Book Club of California, 1960.
        pp. 51, 1 plate   400 copies
        A gold rush memoir written in 1870 for Bancroft's history.
        Ref.: none

609.   **Swisher, James**
         How I Know, or Sixteen Years' Eventful Experience. Cincinnati,
         1880.
         pp. 384, frontis, illus.
Ambushed by Indians in New Mexico, only Swisher and four other
members of the party escaped, the rest being killed. He tells of the
journey into Utah and over the deserts to California.
         Ref.: G-4051, H-S1183

610.   **Taylor, R. R.**
         Seeing the Elephant; Letters of R. R. Taylor, Forty-niner.
Taylor took the Panama route.
         Ref.: none

611.   **Tuttle, E. B.**
         *The Boys' Book about Indians. Being what I saw and Heard for
         Three Years on the Plains.*
Tuttle was Post Chaplain at Ft. Sedgewick and Ft. D. A. Russell in
Wyoming Territory, 1867–70.
         Ref.: G-4221, H-T436

612.   **Tyson, James**
         Diary of a Physician in California.
He tells of traveling from Baltimore to California by schooner.
         Ref.: C-p. 648, H-T451

613.   **Udell, John**   2nd ed.: d, 1946 ed.: a-aa, 1952 ed.: aa
         *Journal of John Udell Kept during a Trip across the Plains, Con-
         taining an Account of the Massacre of a Portion of His Party by
         the Mohave Indians, in 1859* . . . Suisun City: Solano County
         Herald Print, 1859.
         pp. 45, wraps   2 known copies
         2nd ed.: 1868, Jefferson, pp. 48
         rpt.:   1946, Los Angeles, pp. 88; 750 copies; 35 copies
                  signed by Editor Lyle Wright
         rpt.:   1952, New Haven, 200 copies
One of the best known journals of the southern route crossing to
California.
         Ref.: C-p. 649, G-4231, H-U4, WC-346a

614.   **Ward, J. O.**   a
         My Grandpa Went West. Caldwell, 1956.
         pp. 130, frontis in color, e-maps

These are the tales concerning a grandfather who, a week after his marriage in 1849, set out for the gold fields in California. He traveled from Brandenburg, Kentucky to Sacramento by way of Kansas and Colorado.

Ref.: none

615. **Warre, Sir Henry James**
Sketches in North America and the Oregon Territory. By Captain H. Warre . . .
Warre went to Oregon through Canada.
Ref.: G-4543, H-W114, WC-157

616. **Whipple, Amiel W.** b
Report of Explorations . . . from the Mississippi to the Pacific Ocean. Washington: 33rd Congress, 1st Session, House Doc. 129, (Serial 736, 737, 739) (1855).
pp. 154, 2 maps (sizes, 66.5 × 202 cms., 64 × 187 cms.)
Included in House Exec. Doc. 129 with other reports, the subject being Pacific Railroad Explorations. Whipple went overland from Ft. Smith to Los Angeles by the southern trails.
Ref.: H-W340, WC-261

617. **Whipple, Amiel W.** aa
A Pathfinder in the Southwest. The Itinerary of A. W. Whipple during His Explorations . . . in the Years 1853–1854. Edited by Grant Foreman. Norman: University of Oklahoma Press, 1941.
pp. 298, f-map, illus.
Perhaps the most useful book for those interested in Whipple's exploration throughout the southwest part of the country.
Ref.: none

618. **White, Elijah**
A Concise View of Oregon Territory . . .
Even though White was sent overland by the Board of Missions in 1837, and again made the trip in 1842, this time with Medorem Crawford, L. Hastings, and Fitzpatrick as guide, this seventy-two page book deals almost entirely with the Territory's civil matters.
Ref.: G-4628, H-W349, WC-144

619. **Wilkes, Charles**
Narrative of the United States Exploring Expedition during the years 1838 . . . 1842.
The first U.S. exploration of the Northwest part of the country by sea.
Ref.: C-p. 683, H-W414

620.   **Willcox, R. N.**
              Reminiscences of California Life.
              Willcox recounts a voyage to California by Panama.
                  Ref.: C-p. 684, H-W436

621.   **Wilson, Elijah**
              Among the Shoshones.
              Another book described by some as containing reminiscences of an
              overland trip by ox train. This is nowhere to be found in this book,
              the only reference being the opening sentence which reads, "I came
              to Utah in 1850 with my parents when I was a very small boy."
                  Ref.: G-4702, H-W520

622.   **Wilson, Obed G.**
              My Adventures in the Sierras.
              Wilson went to California by way of Nicaragua.
                  Ref.: C-p. 689, G-4707, H-W533

623.   **Wood, Harvey**   aa
              Personal Recollections. Pasadena: pvt. ptg., 1955.
                  pp. 27, e-maps, illus.   200 copies
              Originally twelve copies were printed in 1896 by the "Mountain Echo"
              Job Printing Office in Angels Camp, California. Only two of these
              are known to exist. Of this edition, 100 copies were for members of
              the Zamorano Club, 100 copies for sale. Wood was a member of a
              group calling themselves the Kit Carson Associates. They traveled the
              Gila River along the southern route. Printed as "Scraps of California
              I."
                  Ref.: none

624.   **Woods, Daniel B.**
              Sixteen Months at the Gold Diggings . . .
              A narrative about Woods's voyage to the coast.
                  Ref.: C-p. 694, G-4741, H-W651

625.   **Woods, Rev. James**
              Recollections of Pioneer Work in California . . .
              This recounts Woods's journey around the Horn. Published in 1878.
                  Ref.: C-p. 694

626.   **Wright, Bessie L.**
Diary of a Member of the First Pack Train to Leave Fort Smith for California in 1849.
A diary of Wright's journey through Colorado from Taos, ending soon after they reached Wyoming. Reprinted from the Panhandle-Plains Historical Review in 1969 by the Palo Duro Press.
Ref.: none

627.   **Young, Frank**
Across the Plains in '65.
Young traveled to Pike's Peak.
Ref.: G-4787, H-Y25

Appendix B

Alphabetical Listing
by Year of Travel

1848

Adams, W. L.	6	LemFrit, Honoré-	
Belknap, Keturah	30	Timothée	290
Burrows, Rufus	67	Miller, Jacob	333
Cook, Phineas W.	103	Root, Riley	399
Cornwall, Bruce	107	Simpson, Henry	425
Foster, George G.	160	Stout, Hosea	448
Johnson, Benjamin Franklin			
	258		

1849

Arms, Cephas	14	Egan, Howard	194
Armstrong, J. Elza	404	Fairchild, Lucius	146
Babcock, Leonard	193	Foster, Charles	159
Ball, Nicholas	20	(the) Foster family	161
Banks, Edwin	404	Geiger, Vincent Eply and	
Berrien, Joseph Waring	227	Wakeman Bryarly	173
Bidlack, Russel Eugene	34	Gibson, J. Watt	176
Bigler, Henry W.	194	Goldsmith, Oliver	181
"Boone Emigrant"	509	Goughnour, Emanuel	183
Booth, Edmund	43	Gould, Charles	208
Bristol, C. C.	51	Graham, Martha	
Brooks, E. W.	53	Morgan	187, 337
Brown, James S.	194	Gray, Charles Glass	188
Brown, Joseph	61	Hale, Israel F.	197
Brown, Judge H. S.	193	Hale, John	198
Brown, John E.	59	Hall, John B.	200
Brown, Joseph	61	Hall, Thomas Wakeman	201
Browne, John E.	41	Hamelin, Joseph P.	193
Bruff, J. Goldsborough	64	Hamilton, W. T.	205
Caldwell, Dr. (T. G.?)	73	Hanson, D. M.	209
Carstarphen, James Eula	80	Haun, Catherine	216
Clark, Bennett C.	93	Hayes, Benjamin	219
Clark, Sterling B. F.	95	Haynes, Asa	141
Clifton, John	395	Hickman, William A.	225
Cross, Osborne	112, 414	Hill, Jasper S.	226
Dameron, James Palatine	115	Hindman, David	228
Day, Gershom and		Hinman, Charles G.	229
Elizabeth	468	Hutchings, James Mason	249
Decker, Peter	120	Isham, Giles S.	254
Delano, Alonzo	121	Johnson, Theodore T.	260
De Milt, Alonzo	122	Johnston, William G.	261
Disturnell, John	128	Josselyn, Amos Piatt	264
Dundass, Samuel R.	133	Kellogg, George J.	268

1850

Child, Andrew	88	Loomis, Leander V.	302
Christy, Thomas	90	Lord, Elizabeth	304
Clapp, John T.	92	Loveland, Cyrus C.	307
Coke, Henry J.	100	McGee, Joseph Hedger	317
Davis, Henry T.	116	McKeeby, Lemuel Clarke	320
Davis, Sarah	233	McKinstry, Byron N.	321
Enos, A. A.	143	Maynard, David S. and	
Ferguson, Charles D.	143	Catherine T.	382
Fish, Joseph	153	Moorman, Madison	335
Flake, Lucy Hannah		Newton, John Marshall	344
White	156	Parsons, Lucena	233
Frink, Margaret	166, 233	Peacock, William	360
(A) Georgian	174	Pigman, Walter	370
Gibbs, Mifflin W.	175	Read, George Willis	386
Gill, William	177	Sawyer, Lorenzo	403
Given, Abraham	180	Shaw, David Augustus	419
Goodridge, Sophia Lois	233	Shepherd, Dr. J. S.	421
Hamblin, Jacob	202	Slater, Nelson	426
Hayden, Mary J.	218	Smith, C. W.	428
Hayes, George Edward	220	Soretore, Abram	431
Heywood, Martha Spence	223	Starr, Jeremiah	435
Hinde, Edmund Cavileer	362	Steed, Thomas	437
Hubbard, Chauncey B.	242	Steele, John	438
Ingalls, Eleazar S.	251	Street, Franklin	449
Keller, George	267	Thissell, G. W.	460
Kilgore, William H.	273	Udell, John	473
Lane, Samuel A.	283	Wood, John	504
Langsworthy, Franklin	284	Wooster, David	508
Lee, L. W.	288	Zumwalt, Solomon	513

1851

Alden, Wyllis	152	Crawford, Charles H.	109
Baker, Jean Rio	234	Denny, Arthur A.	123, 486
Booth, William	45	Harris, Sarah Hollister	213
Buckingham, Harriet		Hadley, Amelia	234
Talcott	234	Lobenstine, William C.	296
Cain, Joseph and Brower,		Lockhart, Mrs. Freeman	411
Arieh C.	72	Riddle, George W.	392
Chambers, Margaret W.	86	Williams, Loraine	234
Cranston, Susan Amelia	234	Wood, Elizabeth	234, 503
Churchill, Owen			
Humphrey	385		

1852

1853

Bailey, Washington	16	Kimball, Adelia A.	274
Baker, George Holbrook	17	Kirby, William	278
Beeson, John	28	Knight, Mrs. Amelia	
Belshaw, George	31	Stewart	280
Bixby, Llewellyn	38	Lewis, Capt. John I.	292
Booth, John	44	Longsworth, Basil N.	301
Brown, William Richard	63	Looney, Mrs. M. A.	303
Bushnell, John C.	70	Love, Helen M.	
Campbell, Remembrance		(Stewart)	306
H.	76	Lyman, Esther	309
Cipriani, Leonetto	91	McClure, Andrew S.	313
Cornaby, Hannah	106	Mossman, Isaac	339
Davis, John E.	117	Owen, Benjamin Franklin	352
Dinwiddie, (David or		Parker, Basil G.	358
John)	127	Pengra, Charlotte Stearns	363
Drake, F. M.	129	Piercy, Frederick H.	369
Draper, Elias J.	130	Remy, Jules and	
Ellmaker, Enos	142	Julius Brenchley	389
Fletcher, Daniel C.	157	Stewart, Agnes (Warner)	445
Goltra, Elizabeth Julia	182	Tarbell, J.	455
Hamilton, Mrs. S.		Ward, Dillis B.	480
Watson	204	Ward, Harriet Sherill	481
Handsaker, Samuel	207	Washburn, Catherine	
Ivins, Virginia Wilcox	255	Amanda S.	483
Jones, Rev. Thomas L.	263	West, Calvin B.	491
Judson, Phoebe G.	265	Williams, Wellington	499
Kennedy, George W.	271	Woodworth, James	506

1854

Blood, Jane Wilkie H.	40	Kirkpatrick, Thomas	
Drumheller, "Uncle Dan"	132	Jefferson	279
Francl, Joseph	162	Nobles, William H.	346
Franklin, John Benjamin	163	Nott, Manfred Allen	348
Hunt, Nancy A.		Oaks, George Washington	351
(Zumwalt)	246	Richey, James	391
Huntington, O. B.	248	Steele, John	438, 439
Ingalls, Capt. Rufus	252	Welch, John Allen	490

1855

Chandless, William	87		
Guerin, Mrs. E. J.	192		
Waters, L. M.	484		

1856

Ault, Gertrude M.	82	Judd, Camilla W.	82
Brown, J. Robert	56	Linford, James Henry	294
Burton, Mary	443	Powers, Mary Rockwood	376
Chislett, Mr.	442	Powers, W. P.	377
Cropper, Thomas W.	111	Romney, Miles P.	398
Cunningham, George	82	Stenhouse, Mrs. T. B. H.	443
Jones, Daniel W.	262		

1857

Bandel, Eugene	21	Hamilton, Henry S.	203
Brown, John	58	Horton, Emily	
Buckskin, Mose	365	McGowan	239, 240
Carpenter, Helen	342	Maxwell, William A.	329
Cumming, Elizabeth	113	Perrie, George W.	365
Gove, Capt. Jesse A.	185		

1858

Farmer, J. E.	147	"Utah"	474
Kenderdine, T. S.	270	Wadsworth, William	476
Seville, William P.	415		

1859

Baker, Hozial H.	18	Knight, William Henry	375
Barnett, Joel	22	Marcy, Randolph B.	326
Brown, James Berry	57	Mathews, Edward J.	327
Casler, Melyer	84	Stockton, William J.	447
Evans, Robley D.	145	True, Charles Frederick	470
Greely, Horace	189	West, Simeon H.	493
Kingman, Henry	277		

1860

Batty, Joseph	25	Hawkins, Thomas Samuel	217
Bemis, Stephen A.	32	Lyman, Vincent P.	310
Burton, Sir Richard F.	68	Nibley, Charles Wilson	345
Crane, Ellery P.	108	Porter, Lavinia	
Fjeld, Carl Johan E.	155	Honeyman	373
Fuller, Mrs. Emeline L.	168	Rigdon, Winfield Taylor	393
Hafen, Mrs. Mary Ann		Stucki, John S.	452
(Stucki)	196		

1861

Lander, Frederick West	282
Paup, Harrison	144

1862

Boquist, Mrs. Laura		Nye-Starr, Kate	350
Brewster	46	Redfield, Francis M.	387
Bristol, Rev. Sherlock	52	Smedley, William	427
Hewitt, Randall H.	222	Tourtillott, Jane Gould	467
McComas, E. S.	314	Waite, Catherine Van	
McLaughlin, Daniel	323	Valkenburg	478

1863

Campbell, J. L.	75
Edgerton, Mary	138
Scoville, Adaline Ballou	408

1864

Argyle, Archie	13	Hall, Edward H.	199
Clinkinbeard, Philura V.	98	Harter, George	214
Collins, John	102	Hobson, Mary Quinn	131
Dickson, Albert Jerome	126	Larimer, Mrs. Sarah	285
Dunham, E. Allene		Lomas, Thomas J.	298
Taylor	134	Luster, Mary R.	308
Dunlop, Kate	136	Welty, Mary Jane and	
Fulton, Arabella	169	John	338

Appendix C

Additional Reading

A number of excellent books have been written that are helpful as guidebooks to those interested in literally following the trail from Independence, Missouri, or one of the other "jumping-off" places, to its denouement in Oregon. The origin towns for the emigrants were numerous, as were the many sibling routes that led to, or (subsequent to the crossing of South Pass) away from, the main trail. To undertake the study of these many trail variations is, in itself, a lengthy and somewhat complex project. For those interested in more information regarding the Overland Trail experience today, along with its many secondary roads and cutoffs, the following books are recommended:

1. Clark, Keith and Lowell Tiller. *Terrible Trail: The Meek Cutoff, 1845.* Caldwell, Idaho, 1966.
2. Franzwa, Gregory M. *Maps of the Oregon Trail.* Gerald, Mo.: Patrice Press, 1982.
3. Franzwa, Gregory M. *The Oregon Trail Revisited.* Gerald, Mo.: Patrice Press, 1978.
4. Haines, Aubrey L. *Historic Sites Along the Oregon Trail.* Gerald, Mo.: Patrice Press, 1981.
5. Helfrich, Devere and Helen, and Thomas Hunt, compilers. *Emigrant Trails West.* Klamath Falls, Oregon, 1984.
6. Mattes, Merrill. *The Great Platte River Road.* Nebraska State Historical Society, 1969.
7. Nevada Historical Society. *The Overland Emigrant Trail to California. A Guide to Trail Markers Placed in Western Nevada and the Sierra Nevada Mountains of California.* Reno, Nevada, 1980.
8. Paden, Irene. *Prairie Schooner Detours.* New York: McMillan & Co., 1949.

9. Paden, Irene. *Wake of the Prairie Schooner*. New York: McMillan & Co., 1943.

The above should serve as a tempting entree for many other articles and publications concerning the subject.

Index